# The Wild Robot

## SQ0100 - THE PROLOGUE

DREAMWORKS OPENING SEQUENCE SETTLES ON A MOON

DISSOLVE to a darker version. Storm clouds blanket the moon, PULSING with lightning.

Sounds of the storm build in ferocity and volume, the thunder reaches a crescendo.

                                        SMASH TO:

## SQ0200 - THE ROBOT HATCHES

EXT. DESERTED BEACH - DAWN

Blinding daylight, silent save for ocean ripples lapping at a soft stone beach. The sky and shoreline are distorted as if viewed through a wide lens. SLOW PULL-OUT reveals a rugged coast reflected on the rounded lens of a robot, ROZZUM 7134. WIDEN to reveal the Rozzum peers from a rupture in a mostly intact shipping crate.

Otters gather, investigating the curiosity. One POKES at the back of the robot's head, accidentally ACTIVATING it.

                    ROZZUM 7134
         Hello. Bonjour. Guten tag. Hujambo. Hola.
         Congratulations on your purchase of a
         Universal Dynamics robot. I am Rozzum
         seven-one-three-four. A Rozzum always
         completes its task, just ask!

Silence. ROZZUM 7134 blinks.

                  ROZZUM 7134 (CONT'D)
         Just, ask--

Rozzum 7134 is BLINDSIDED by a wave. Rolled under the brine, it is driven like a toy against a basalt wall.

The wave RECEDES, leaving 7134 to drain. Another wave LOOMS.

                  ROZZUM 7134 (CONT'D)
         Processing.

Rozzum 7134 attempts to climb to safety, SLIPS. Rozzum 7134 notes a crab scuttling up the rock wall.

She RECONFIGURES to match the crab's stance. Rozzum 7134 successfully climbs clear.

EXT. CLIFFTOP - MOMENTS LATER

The crab clambers into view, followed by Rozzum 7134.

**ROZZUM VISION: "CUSTOMER LOCATED?"**

      ROZZUM 7134
  Do you need--

The crab is SNATCHED away by a passing gull.

      ROZZUM 7134 (CONT'D)
  ...assistance?

Rozzum 7134 FOCUSES on a wall of thick vegetation before it: deploys sound gathering arrays.

Rozzum 7134 COCKS its head, listening: animal and bird sounds drift through the curtain of greenery.

      ROZZUM 7134 (CONT'D)
  Ready to receive my first task.

Rozzum 7134 pushes into the forest.

## SQ0250 - THE FOREST

EXT. ISLAND FOREST - DAY

ON A RAVEN landing in the branches of a tree. He PAUSES, an unfamiliar sound approaching; MUSIC.

LOOKING DOWN he sees Rozzum 7134 making her way through the trees. Her upper body ROTATING cheerily.

      ROZZUM 7134
  Rozzum Seven One Three Four is available
  for task assignment.

A LYNX PEERS at the passing oddity.

      ROZZUM 7134 (CONT'D)
  Rozzum robots come standard with the
  Alpha-113 dimensional processor.

Rozzum 7134 PASSES through the trees.

                    ROZZUM 7134 (CONT'D)
               If you are unsure about how I can
               assist, try asking me about myself.

On Rozzum 7134 navigating a tilted log in an attempt to
communicate with a BADGER.

                    ROZZUM 7134 (CONT'D)
               Excuse me! Did you know I can
               assist with grocery shopping?
               Banking? Landscaping?

The badger burrows away. 7134 spies a squirrel PEERING
DOWN from its tree house.

                    ROZZUM 7134 (CONT'D)
               Hello! Did you perhaps order a Rozzum
               helper robot?

7134 is PELTED with acorns.

                    ROZZUM 7134 (CONT'D)
               Is that a no?

Rozzum 7134 FLASHES the squirrel unexpectedly with a
chest strobe, BLINDING it. A little WHIRRING sound as a
sticker is dispensed from a small slit in 7134's chest.

                    ROZZUM 7134 (CONT'D)
               Here's a free sticker. Scan the code and
               receive ten percent off of your--

The squirrel RIPS UP the sticker.

ON A BEAVER, PADDLER, finishing a modest dam. He hears
weird music. Spies 7134 WALKING PAST like Bigfoot. 7134
PAUSES, RUNS toward Paddler.

                    ROZZUM 7134 (CONT'D)
               Do you need assistance?

He's PETRIFIED.

                    ROZZUM 7134 (CONT'D)
               I see your problem.

Rozzum 7134 PULLS a key branch. The entire dam collapses -
is washed away.

FLASH! 7134 generates a sticker for Paddler, who
disappears under the water.

ON A DEER BOUNDING through the meadow.

Rozzum 7134 RECONFIGURES TO EMULATE THE DEER'S LEAPS.

> ROZZUM 7134 (CONT'D)
> (LEAPING up alongside)
> Rozzums are programmed for instant physical mimicry, so as to--

The deer VEERS. KICKS Rozzum 7134.

A BUTTERFLY FLITS past her lenses.

Rozzum 7134 APPROACHES a tree surfaced in butterflies.

ALL the insects FLY at once. Surrounded in a cloud of color and movement, Rozzum 7134 is disoriented.

A butterfly LANDS on her finger.

A RAVEN lands, CRUSHES the butterfly in its beak.

A Lynx LEAPS from cover, ATTACKING the raven on 7134's hand. Rozzum 7134 EXTENDS her arm a bit, distancing her head from the savage battle at the end of her arm.

> ROZZUM 7134 (CONT'D)
> Aggression detected.

A wolverine GRABS the other half of the dead raven, a savage TUG-OF-WAR over its body.

The raven's head POPS off and lands in 7134's hand.

> ROZZUM 7134 (CONT'D)
> My communication package includes strategies for conflict resolution.

The fight is ESCALATING quickly. Dust OBSCURES the scene.

A skunk, DAISY, rumbles into the fray. The fight is instantly quenched, the aggressors FLEE. 7134 PICKS UP the skunk.

The skunk BERATES 7134 savagely.

> ROZZUM 7134 (CONT'D)
> Your dialect is not in my databanks.

7134 places the skunk back on the ground.

> ROZZUM 7134 (CONT'D)
> Tell your people not to worry. Rozzum 7134 will sort out this language barrier in no time.

The skunk SPRAYS. The noxious cloud ENVELOPS 7134.

EXT. FOREST - LATER

CLOSE ON 7134'S HEAD - she is sitting very still.

                    ROZZUM 7134
        Activating learning mode.

PULL BACK, revealing we are in TIME LAPSE. Nights and days pass, with a multitude of animals stopping by. Rain falls, leaves litter her. Rozzum 7134 never moves. A WEEK passes, leaves gathering on her exterior. Animals ignore her, go about their business. 7134's processor GRINDS AWAY. DING!

**ROZZUM VISION: TRANSLATION COMPLETE**

                    WEASEL 2
        Hey, check it out. Look, look, look.
        Somebody died over here.

                    WEASEL 3
        Lemme see, lemme see. Oooh.

                    WEASEL 2
        Who was it?

                    WEASEL 1
        Anybody we know?

                    WEASEL 2
        Fresh or not fresh?

                    WEASEL 1
        Smells pretty good.

                    WEASEL 2
        Tastes terrible.

                    WEASEL 3
        Oh, it's waking up! Run!

                    WEASEL 2
        Hey it's waking up!

                    WEASEL 1
        It's a monster! Run for your lives!

Rozzum 7134 RISES, brushing debris off of herself.

EXT. CLEARING - LATER.

A multitude of animals graze, forage, flit here and there. They all STOP. Rozzum 7134 strides out into the open.

> PADDLER
> Look! That's the thing that destroyed my dam.

> ANIMALS
> The monster! Yikes! I think it's gonna talk.

> ROZZUM 7134
> Thank you for your patience while I deciphered your language. I am Rozzum seven one three four, ready to enhance your lives with integrated multi-phased task accomplishment.

A SUPER CUTE bunny baby HOPS UP.

> BABY BUNNY
> Are you here to kill us?

> ROZZUM 7134
> Negative, I am here to help with whatever tasks you-

> BABY BUNNY
> (to the crowd)
> It says no.

> BROADFOOT (O.S.)
> *SNORT*

Roz is RUN DOWN by a huge moose, BROADFOOT.

> BROADFOOT (CONT'D)
> It's dead.

> ANIMAL CROWD
> Oh, thank goodness.

7134 RISES AGAIN, like a haunted marionette.

REELING IN her arms and legs: the sight is weird, unsettling.

> ANIMAL CROWD (CONT'D)
> AAAAAAAAAAUGHHHHHHHHH. The monster!

The animals SCATTER. Rozzum 7134 is left alone.

                    ROZZUM 7134
               Did anyone order me?


EXT. MOUNTAIN PEAK - DUSK

Rozzum 7134 has a 360 degree view. ORBIT to describe an
island: no other land or structures in sight. She's
TRAPPED on an ISLAND.

                    ROZZUM 7134
               ...anyone?

No responses.

                    ROZZUM 7134 (CONT'D)
               Delivery unsuccessful. Return to factory.
               Activating return transmitter.

From Rozzum 7134's head, a greenish rod RISES - the
TRANSMITTER.

A DOWNPOUR STRIKES. Rozzum 7134 POWERS UP the
transmitter. It LIGHTS as the charge builds:
red...yellow...GREEN!

                    ROZZUM 7134 (CONT'D)
               Three, two, one--

BOOM! Rozzum 7134 is hit by lightning. She FALLS from the
summit.


## SQ0600 - THE ACCIDENT


EXT. FOREST - NIGHT

ON ROZZUM 7134 lying motionless and dark.

**ROZZUM VISION: OVER A BLACK SCREEN -** *"SYSTEM BOOTING.
ACCESS PANEL BREACH. PANEL 10 OPEN. PANEL 28 OPEN. PANEL
11, 51, 32 OPEN."*

Rozzum 7134 POWERS UP. Her eye covers CLICK open to
reveal--

She is missing an eye and a hand.

ON HER TORSO - a multitude of access panels flap open.
PAN to find the ground is strewn with paper manuals,
small tools. TILT UP to find *raccoons making off with
Rozzum 7134's stuff.*

Lightning FLASHES. Rozzum 7134 hurries to retrieve all her lost items. As quickly as she can gather them, other raccoons try and take them back.

In one tug-of-war, a raccoon accidentally UNPLUGS a black box. Its exposed contacts SIZZLE with power, and Rozzum 7134 is ZAPPED.

Understanding the power he yields, the raccoon GRINS and runs off with his new weapon.

Feeling overwhelmed, Rozzum 7134 tries DEPLOYING her transmitter again.

                   ROZZUM 7134
    Activating return transmitter. Three.

                   RACCOONS
 Ooooooh.

                   RACCOONS (CONT'D)
 Pretty.

                   RACCOONS (CONT'D)
 Get it.

                   ROZZUM 7134
 Two...

Attracted to the shiny transmitter, the raccoons SWARM Rozzum 7134 to get to it.

                   ROZZUM 7134 (CONT'D)
 One...

One raccoon manages to POP it out.

                   RACCOON
 Ha!

The raccoon heads STRAIGHT UP A PINE, CHASED by the raccoon hoard and Rozzum 7134.

                   RACCOONS
 Come back.

They near the top - the tree BENDING under their weight. Arcing down, the top of the tree lands on a rocky ledge.

                   RACCOON
 Wait, stop! No!

Rozzum 7134 STANDS and CHASES after the transmitter.

                              RACCOONS
                    No no no no no!

Releasing the tree top from her weight, the tree trunk
SNAPS back upright, FLINGING a hundred raccoons into the
night sky. They splash down in the ocean.

                              RACCOON
                    Again!

The raccoon with the transmitter DISAPPEARS into a cave.
Moments later he RETREATS, WITHOUT the transmitter.
Rozzum 7134 REACHES INTO the cave to retrieve it, but a
huge grizzly, THORN, STEPS over it.

                              THORN
                         (sfx)
                    Growling.

Thorn STRIKES Rozzum 7134 mid-chest. Claws dig deep
grooves - SPARKS FLY from her seams.

Rozzum 7134 RETREATS, power intermittent. Thorn closes.

**ROZZUM VISION: A confusion of trees punctuated by
blinding lightning flashes.**

Rozzum 7134 BUMPS into a tree. She SLIPS, TUMBLING CLEAR
of Thorn, heading downhill, knocking small trees flat.

Rozzum 7134 lays still, tangled in branches, caked with
mud. Dwindling rain PATS her metal body.

7134 OPENS her main panel. Inside are equivalents of
bones, arteries, lungs, and a heart. Everything GLOWS
with tracing energy save for the heart, which is dark.
Rozzum 7134 TAPS it. A few PULSES, then nothing.

7134 CLOSES the panel, finds a feather stuck to the
outside. Examining it, she sees a similar spray of
feathers peeking through the debris beneath her. She
gently grasps them, pulling a limp wing into view. Death
is abstract to Rozzum 7134, she shows no emotion.

Letting go of the wing, she carefully wipes away the
branches to reveal a group of SHATTERED EGG SHELLS.

7134 lifts shell fragments, pieces them together. Then
something catches her gaze...Rozzum 7134 moves some
leaves away to REVEAL... ONE INTACT EGG.

**ROZZUM VISION: Infrared scan reveals a living bird
within.**

She lifts it, very carefully indeed.

## SQ0700 - THE EGG AND THE FOX

EXT. HOLLOW - MOMENTS LATER

Rozzum 7134 sits, considering the egg and her transmitter.

7134 GLANCES away, looks back to find the egg is GONE.

The dense foliage RUSTLES as something small makes their escape.

**ROZZUM VISION:** Switching to INFRARED Rozzum 7134 locates the creature, gives CHASE.

>                    ROZZUM 7134
>           May I confirm that is yours?

The egg is with a red fox, FINK. He is wily and slick. Even when 7134 gets him by the tail, he slithers free.

Fink shelters in a log. 7134 SPLITS IT with a SAW. She retrieves the egg, STASHES it in a storage compartment.

Fink PRIES OPEN a back panel, RECOVERS his EGG.

Fink rockets into a thicket, an EVIL GRIN on his face. Rozzum 7134 closes: the brush abruptly CLEARS and Rozzum 7134 FALLS off the edge of a cliff.

Fink strides out on a limb, satisfied: he drew Rozzum 7134 here deliberately. Rozzum 7134's cabled hand SHOOTS UP and GRASPS the limb. Rozzum 7134 REELS IN her extended arm. VAULTING OVER Fink, she lands back on the cliff edge.

Surprised, cut off on the branch and out of options, Fink RELINQUISHES the egg.

>                    FINK
>           Here you go. Take it.

As Rozzum 7134 reaches for the egg, Fink SWALLOWS it.

Rozzum 7134 GRABS Fink by the neck, SQUEEZES the egg out of him. The egg FLIES over Rozzum 7134's head. Fink DASHES between her legs, LEAPS, CATCHES the egg mid-air, and then LANDS straight on top of a porcupine.

Fink DROPS the egg. Rozzum 7134 recovers it intact.

The porcupine RETREATS, leaving Fink to deal with a face-full of quills. He's unable to dislodge even one.

To his surprise, Rozzum 7134 PICKS HIM UP, and quickly uses a tool to pluck the quills out.

She sets him back down.

Fink SNARLS and dashes for cover.

## SQ0800 - THE EGG HATCHES

EXT. DEEP FOREST - LATER

ON ROZZUM 7134, a RATTLING from her interior. She removes the egg. Examines it.

'CRACK' - the egg has a HAIRLINE RUPTURE.

Rozzum 7134 gently PINCHES the shell to close it up. More cracks form. Rozzum 7134 FRANTICALLY tries to hold it all together. For a moment, it works.

The egg EXPLODES. A tiny gosling sits in Rozzum 7134's palm.

> GOSLING
> Peep?

The new gosling LOOKS UP, into Rozzum 7134's glowing blue eyes. Something wordlessly passes between them. The gosling places his forehead against Rozzum 7134. Her subsurface lights GLOW powerfully.

The magic moment is interrupted when 7134 callously PLUCKS UP the gosling, sets it back on the ground.

> ROZZUM 7134
> Was this task accomplished to your satisfaction?

The gosling SCREAMS. FLASH. Rozzum 7134 STICKS a sticker to his chest.

> ROZZUM 7134 (CONT'D)
> On a scale of one to ten where ten is most satisfied and one is least, how would you rate my performance?

> GOSLING
> Peep.

Rozzum 7134 hands the gosling a sticker.

                    ROZZUM 7134
          I will register that as a 'ten'.

Rozzum 7134 attempts to activate her transmitter.

                    ROZZUM 7134 (CONT'D)
          Returning to factory.

The transmitter BLINKS, unstable.

                    ROZZUM 7134 (CONT'D)
          Signal strength weak. Seeking higher
          ground.

Rozzum 7134 STRIDES AWAY.

                    GOSLING
          *peep peep peep*

The gosling RACES after her. For every step Rozzum 7134 takes, the gosling must dash thirty or more.

                    ROZZUM 7134
          Do you require shelter?

Rozzum 7134 covers the gosling with a piece of wood. As she walks, the wood TRAILS behind 7134.

Rozzum 7134 STRIDES into the forest. The gosling HOPS onto her foot, riding along. Roz stops, a DING! Her center compartment opens.

                    ROZZUM 7134 (CONT'D)
          Perhaps tips for planning your next
          vacation?

She sets a travel pamphlet on the ground: FLORIDA - MORE SHORELINE THAN EVER - and continues on her way. The gosling FALLS DOWN A HOLE. Moments later, the gosling TODDLES out onto a branch beside Rozzum 7134, HOPPING ONTO her shoulder. The gosling SNUGGLES under Rozzum 7134's chin.

                    ROZZUM 7134 (CONT'D)
          I do not understand this response.

Rozzum 7134's transmitter lights up.

                    ROZZUM 7134 (CONT'D)
          Signal acquired. Three, two, one--

The gosling PECKS the transmitter. BREAKS it.

BABY OPOSSUM 1(OS)
Mom, I don't feel good.

## SQ1000 - THE TASK

A rustling in the brush. Roz INVESTIGATES, sees a opossum mother, PINKTAIL, with four baby opossums on her back.

BABY OPOSSUM 1
If I barf, I'm taking you all with me.

BABY OPOSSUM 2
Mom told you not to eat grasshoppers, dummy.

BABY OPOSSUM 3
Petunia's been in front all day.

BABY OPOSSUM 4
The prettiest opossum always rides in front.

BABY OPOSSUM 3
Try being pretty with my tail jammed in your eye.

Rozzum 7134's hand SETS the gosling on the back of Pinktail.

BABY OPOSSUMS
(blood-curdling)
**EEEEEEEEEEEEEEEEEK**.

Pinktail STANDS, SPILLING the babies.

PINKTAIL
Bartlett, stop jamming your tail in your sister's eye.

BABY OPOSSUM 4
I'm Rowan. Bartlett was last litter.

PINKTAIL
Are you sure? Who are all of you? Go away.

BABY OPOSSUM 4
We're your children. Except for him.

GOSLING
*Peep*

Pinktail is astonished to see her brood has grown by one.

                PINKTAIL
This is what I get for taking a walk. Where's your mommy, little guy?

Pinktail notices Roz PEERING at them.

                PINKTAIL (CONT'D)
The <u>monster</u>. AAAAAAAAAAUGHHHHHHH.

Pinktail and the babies KEEL OVER.

                BABY OPOSSUM 5
        (dramatic)
*cough cough*

                BABY OPOSSUM 4
        (whisper)
You gotta die faster.

                BABY OPOSSUM 5
Meningitis takes a while.

                BABY OPOSSUM 6
What did you pick?

                BABY OPOSSUM 7
Rabies.

                BABY OPOSSUM 8
Spontaneous combustion!

                BABY OPOSSUM 4
Nightshade salad.

                BABY OPOSSUM 9
Sepsis.

                BABY OPOSSUMS
Hey! <u>I</u> picked sepsis!

                PINKTAIL
<u>None of you are doing it right</u>. We talked about this. Dead things don't have to explain why they're dead. Now we're gonna get killed for real.

                BABY OPOSSUMS
        (together)
Sorry mom.

                    BABY OPOSSUM
                  (a beat late)
              Sorry.

Beat.

                    BABY OPOSSUM 4
              Why aren't we killed yet?

                    PINKTAIL
              Good question.

Pinktail parts the foliage to investigate. Roz has rolled away. The gosling scampers up and PERCHES on Rozzum 7134's shoulder. The sight emboldens Pinktail to crawl up to investigate.

                    BABY OPOSSUM 2
              Nice knowing you, mom.

                    PINKTAIL
                  (to the gosling)
              Alright, it's ok. It's ok.

Pinktail PEERS into Rozzum 7134's body cavity.

                    PINKTAIL (CONT'D)
              Uh, hey. You in there? I'm Pinktail.

Rozzum 7134's head partially emerges from her body.

                    PINKTAIL (CONT'D)
              Ok. Hello. This gosling is yours?

                    BABY OPOSSUM 3
              Wow.

Rozzum 7134 hands the gosling back to Pinktail.

                    ROZZUM 7134
              Negative. That gosling stalks me, emits
              noise, and makes simple tasks more
              complicated or impossible.

                    PINKTAIL
              Yeah, they do that. Goslings imprint on
              the first thing they see. Which would be
              you.

                    BABY OPOSSUM 6
              <u>Congratulations</u>.

                    PINKTAIL
          As far as he's concerned, you're his
          mother now.

                    ROZZUM 7134
          I do not have the programming to be a
          mother.

Rozzum 7134 walks away.

                    BABY OPOSSUMS (O.S.)
          It's gonna squish us!

Pinktail ambushes her, DROPPING down from a branch.

                    PINKTAIL
          No one does. We just make it up.

                    ROZZUM 7134
          Without an assigned task, my next
          priority is to return to factory.

                    PINKTAIL
          Taking care of him is your task now.

Pinktail said the magic word: TASK. A CHIME sounds. MUSIC
PLAYS. Tracer lights activate:

                    ROZZUM 7134
          Task _acquired_. Return mode delayed. A
          Rozzum always completes its task.

As Pinktail talks, her babies BITE, CHEW, and FIGHT with
each other. The mother opossum uses her prehensile tail
to separate them, smack them, etc.

                    PINKTAIL
          You're lucky you just have one. As a
          mother of seven--

                    BABY OPOSSUM (O.S.)
          AAAAAAAAAAAAAAAAAAAAUGHHHHHH.

                    PINKTAIL
          ...Six babies, it's a full time thing.

She picks up one of the babies.

                    PINKTAIL (CONT'D)
          But it's not _all_ bad.

The baby BARFS up a hairball.

PINKTAIL (CONT'D)
          Just mostly bad.

                    ROZZUM 7134
          Do you have any information on how to
          take care of this unit?

                    PINKTAIL
          They all need to eat. But yours needs to
          swim, and fly. Fly by fall. He's gotta
          leave this island before winter, or, how
          do I put this delicately?

                    BABY OPOSSUMS
          Aaaaaaaughhhhh.

The opossum babies all FEIGN GRISLY DEATH.

                    PINKTAIL
          Yeah. That.

                    ROZZUM 7134
          Eat. Swim. Fly by fall. Or aaaaugh.

                    PINKTAIL
          Patience is the key.

A CHEWED UP baby appears.

                    BABY OPOSSUM 4
          It's okay mom, I'm alive.

                    PINKTAIL (O.S.)
                (flat)
          Oh. Yay. Well, good luck.

Babies CLIMB ONTO Pinktail's back. Pinktail walks away.

                    BABY OPOSSUMS
          Goodbye. We like your new baby. Hope it
          doesn't die.


## SQ1100 - THE HUNGRY GOSLING


EXT. MEADOW - MORNING

Rozzum 7134 PROJECTS images of people EATING, diagram of a person SWIMMING and a Jet aircraft FLYING.

                    ROZZUM 7134
          Eat. Swim. Fly by fall.

Her gaze DRIFTS from the image to focus on the gosling on her shoulder.

FINK'S POV - watching Rozzum 7134 and the gosling.

CUT TO:

EXT. GLEN - LATER

Rozzum 7134 holds a pinecone in one hand, the gosling in the other.

                      ROZZUM 7134
    Eat.

She tries to plug the pinecone into the gosling's mouth. It is FAR too big.

                      FINK
    Huh.

EXT. PONDSIDE - LATER

ON THE GOSLING still staring lovingly at Rozzum 7134, as she PUSHES him out into the pond afloat a pinecone.

                      ROZZUM 7134
    Swim.

The gosling TODDLES back to Rozzum 7134, FALLING from the pinecone and INSTANTLY SINKING.

Paddler SURFACES, the gosling on his tail.

                      PADDLER
    I say, keep your trash out of my pond.
    That's littering. Not to mention murder.

He LAUNCHES the gosling back.

The gosling SNUGGLES back in its little spot under her chin.

EXT. FIELD - LATER

The gosling stands in the center of 7134's hand. Rozzum 7134 retracts her palm. As it gazes lovingly at her, she ACTIVATES it.

                      ROZZUM 7134
    Fly.

In a blink it is three hundred feet in the air. A passing falcon SNATCHES it.

ON THE SMILING GOSLING in 7134's palm. She is FLUMMOXED how to proceed. CORRECT to find Fink, sitting right there.

                FINK
Allow me to introduce myself. Fink. Predator and local goose expert. Which I know <u>you</u> could use about now.

Rozzum 7134 SNATCHES the gosling clear of Fink.

                ROZZUM 7134
<u>You are the destroyer unit.</u>

                FINK
It's okay, I won't eat him.

Rozzum 7134 IMMEDIATELY sets the gosling back where it was.

                FINK (CONT'D)
Are you crazy, I might eat him.

                ROZZUM 7134
You said you would not.

                FINK
Do you believe everything you hear?

                ROZZUM 7134
Yes.

Fink's eyes WIDEN.

                FINK
Noted.

                ROZZUM 7134
Why did you steal my gosling?

                FINK
I'm a fox. I do foxy things. It's in my nature.

                ROZZUM 7134
Your, programming.

                FINK
Why'd you help me?

ROZZUM 7134
I'm a robot. I do robotty things. I seek tasks and ensure all essential needs have been met or exceeded.

Rozzum 7134 gives Fink a tablet. He scrolls through marvelous images of pools, houses, and GREAT FEASTS. Fink DIGS at the screen, trying to get at the food.

FINK
I have some essential needs.

GOSLING
*Whimpering hungry noises*

ROZZUM 7134
Fink, as a local goose expert, how do I get--
(she holds up the gosling)
--to eat, swim, fly?

FINK
I thought you'd never ask. Let's start with eat.

EXT. FOREST - LATER.

ON SCALLOPS VACUUMED UP

FINK (O.S.)
Yeah, yeah, yeah, right there.

The fresh scallops are arranged around Brightbill. They collectively SNAP SHUT on him. Rozzum 7134 VACUUMS them off the gosling.

ROZZUM 7134
I do not think these are suitable.

FINK
Wait, wait, lemme check.

Roz gives the shellfish to Fink, who swallows them greedily.

FINK (CONT'D)
Ooh. Mmm. Seems good to me.

ON A SWARM OF BEES

FINK (CONT'D)
Say...can You make yourself look like a bear?

Rozzum 7134 imitates Thorn's pose.

> FINK (CONT'D)
> (in Thorn voice)
> I'm here for a honey lunch.

The Bees SWARM her head.

> ROZZUM 7134
> I believe I am under attack.

> FINK
> You're doing great.

7134 LIFTS Fink up to the bees' vacated hive.

> ROZZUM 7134
> Should I be concerned?

> FINK
> (eyeing the honey)
> Sorry, can't hear you.

Fink GORGES himself on the dripping honey then drops some down to the gosling.

> FINK (CONT'D)
> (mouth full)
> Here you go, kid.

The gosling just gets stuck.

KING SALMON STOLEN from Thorn.

ON ROZZUM 7134 RUNNING from a RAMPANT Thorn. Rozzum 7134 carries Fink, who is eating the salmon.

> ROZZUM 7134
> How do goslings normally do this?

## SQ1175 - THE RUNT

EXT. BEACH - EVENING

Rozzum 7134 uses a laser to STEAM clams.

Fink fishes out a clam, gobbling the steaming contents. He's bloated, grotesque, stuffed to bursting.

> ROZZUM 7134
> This is not working.

                    FINK
          Are you kidding? Everything is working
          great.

                    GOSLING
               (whimpering from hunger)

                    FINK
               (seeing starving gosling)
          Oh, yeah that. Here.

Still laying on his back, Fink lazily SCRATCHES AWAY a surface of pebbles, exposing a swarm of grubs.

The gosling EATS. A chime inside Rozzum 7134 SOUNDS.

**ROZZUM VISION: The first of the three gosling icons, the EATING ICON, is marked COMPLETED.**

                    ROZZUM 7134
          Phase one of task is completed.

Rozzum 7134 RELAXES a little. SITS.

                    FINK
          Now, we're gonna have to do all this over
          tomorrow. All these kids do is eat.

                    ROZZUM 7134
          I understand.

Rozzum 7134 OPENS her main hatch, exposing her dark power core.

                    FINK
          What's that?

                    ROZZUM 7134
          My power core. It is damaged. Without it
          I rely on my solar surfaces and
          batteries.

                    FINK
               (still eating)
          Yeah, you should work on that.

                    ROZZUM 7134
          I also need a replacement transmitter.

Rozzum 7134 shows the broken unit to Fink.

                    FINK
          Ugh, do I have to do everything? When we
          run across another robot we'll kill it
          and take its transmitter.

                    ROZZUM 7134
          Negative. Rozzum inhibition protocols
          prevent deliberate harm to others.

ON A crab CHASING the gosling. Rozzum 7134 PLUCKS UP the crab, sends it on its way.

                    FINK
          Look. You need to learn how things work
          on this island.

Fink BLOCKS the crab's exit, DROPS it into the boiling water.

                    FINK (CONT'D)
          Me, the bear, everybody, we're all
          just trying to survive. And
          kindness, is not a survival skill.

Fink watches the awkward gosling. Rozzum 7134 considers as well.

                    FINK (CONT'D)
          Yeah. So, uh, how'd you get a gosling,
          anyways?

                    ROZZUM 7134
          There was an accident. I terminated his
          family.

Fink claps his paws over the gosling's ears.

                    FINK
          For future reference, you probably
          want to keep all that to yourself.

                    ROZZUM 7134
          Understood. Do not mention dead family.
          Fink, how long do you estimate swim and
          fly to take?

                    FINK
          Swimming's easy. I can teach him the way
          my mom taught me. Swim.

Fink BOOTS the gosling out into the ocean. Roz REACHES to retrieve him.

                    ROZZUM 7134
          Fink! He will not learn that way.

                    FINK
          Not if you keep doing that.

He hops onto Rozzum 7134's shoulder.

                    FINK (CONT'D)
          Just between us, this whole thing may not
          take as long as you think. Your gosling,
          he isn't exactly normal.

                    ROZZUM 7134
          I have a defective baby?

                    FINK
          He's what they call a 'runt'.

                    ROZZUM 7134
          A runt.

                    FINK
          Fact is, even if his whole family hadn't
          been killed, he probably wouldn't have
          lived very long. Just, I don't know.
          Don't get too attached to the little guy,
          that's all.

Rozzum 7134 CONSIDERS.

                    FINK (CONT'D)
          If you want, I could eat him right now
          and save you the grief later.

Fink POPS the gosling in his mouth. Rozzum 7134 REACHES down his throat to RETRIEVE it.

                    ROZZUM 7134
          Negative. Eating this task is not the
          same as completing it.

Rozzum 7134 SETS the gosling on her collar. Fink SNATCHES at it. 7134 ROTATES the ring, keeping the gosling clear of Fink's anxious paws.

                    FINK
                (snatching)
          So we're doing this. Well, if you don't
          want me or anyone else to eat him, you're
          going to need a place that's safer than
          out here...
                (an idea dawning)
          which is a great idea! New project!

Rozzum 7134 drags Fink away. He BURPS.

                    FINK (CONT'D)
Is it normal to burp this much?

### SQ1200 - THE LODGE

EXT. BASE OF REDWOOD - MOMENTS LATER

Rozzum 7134, Fink and the Gosling pass nearby, a load of wood in Rozzum 7134's arms. They walk past a BEAVER chewing a MASSIVE REDWOOD.

                    BABY OPOSSUM 2
That thing's gonna fall on you.

                    BABY OPOSSUM 7
And squish you to jelly.

                    SQUIRREL
This guy's nuts.

                    ROZZUM 7134
Who is that?

                    FINK
Paddler? Local laughing stock. Spends every day trying to cut down the biggest tree on the island. He's obsessed. Kind of like you and your task hang up.

                    ROZZUM 7134
His, programming?

                    FINK
     (calling to Paddler)
Hey Paddler. You're never going to finish that.

                    PADDLER
Felling this is not the point. The process is the art.

                    FINK
And that's what happens to your brain when you eat wood. Weirdo.

                    PADDLER
Yeah? Well, you'll eat those words, vermin.

EXT. PADDLER'S LODGE - LATER

Roz scoops up Paddler's lodge.

 ROZZUM 7134
 Are you sure Paddler will not mind us
 borrowing his home?

 FINK
 He doesn't need to know.

EXT. LODGE HOLLOW - LATER

Rozzum 7134 PROJECTS a compact dome over the gosling.

 FINK
 Seriously? He needs room for me and my
 stuff.

7134 ENLARGES the dome substantially.

 FINK (CONT'D)
 Better. Now, you can make one this big,
 right?

 ROZZUM 7134
 No task is impossible for Rozzum Seven
 One Three Four.

 GOSLING (O.S.)
 Roz feffin-nun tree sore.

 ROZ
 But you can call me Roz.

 GOSLING
 Roz. Roz Roz Roz.

EXT. LODGE HOLLOW - LATE AFTERNOON

Roz PILES ROCKS. The gosling HOPS from rock to rock,
making a game of it.

 GOSLING
 Roz! Roz! Roz!

 FINK
 Where are you from that things don't eat
 each other?

 ROZ
 I do not know my origin point.

26.

FINK
Well who made you?

ROZ
Someone made me?

GOSLING
Someone made me?

A group of squirrels LAUGH at Roz' progress.

Fink BEANS them with a mouse.

FINK
Hahahahah.

GOSLING
Hahahahah.

ROZZUM 7134
Humor is based on misfortune?

GOSLING
Missortune.

FINK
Yeah. Here. Try it.

GOSLING
Yeah!

Fink PULLS back a curtain of grass, lining up a rabbit.

A high-velocity pinecone TAKES OUT Fink.

FINK
Not funny.

GOSLING
Not funny. Hahahahah.

Roz weaves branches at lightning speed.

Fink throws a squirrel.

FINK
Ugh. Squirrels.

The gosling RUNS OFF. He PICKS a little branch, runs back, TAPS on Roz' foot.

ROZ
Your inefficient participation will slow the process.

                    GOSLING
          Slow the process. I'll just be over here.
          A little sad, but otherwise okay.

The gosling walks away, sad.

                    ROZ
          Just this once.

Roz LIFTS the gosling, allows it to place its twig. The gosling BEAMS.

FOUR MORE shots of Roz letting the gosling place twigs.

                    GOSLING
          Perfect.

They admire the finished lodge.

                    GOSLING (CONT'D)
          Home?

                    FINK
          A little rustic.

                    ROZ
          I think I know what is missing.

EXT. SHORELINE - AFTERNOON

Roz, Fink, and the gosling search for wood on the beach.

                    FINK
          So what you gonna name him?

                    ROZ
          I assign to you Gosling zero-zero-zero-one.

Roz glows proudly.

                    FINK
          Ok. That sucked.

                    GOSLING
          That sucked.

BOOM. Thunder rumbles over the beach.

EXT. FOREST - LATER

Roz, Fink, and the gosling huddle under a tree to escape the storm.

          FINK
     You gotta learn to just make stuff up.
     Come on, find that 'AWOOOO' inside you.

Roz OPENS a panel, PEERS inside.

          ROZ
     Searching. "A W O O O O..."

          GOSLING
     Aaaa woo ooo ooo ooo--

Fink NOTES the strangeness.

          FINK
     Anything yet?

          ROZ
     No.

          FINK
     Just have a little fun for once?

          ROZ
     'Gosling zero-one-eight-six.' There. You
     see what I did? His numbering is out of
     sequence. 'Waaaaaaaaah.'

Fink glares. Beans a laughing squirrel.

## SQ1300 - THE BEDTIME STORY

INT. LODGE - EVENING

Roz BURNS images onto a piece of wood.

          FINK
     His name can't have numbers. It's like
     someone didn't even like him.

Roz places it on the mantel. She stands back, revealing a series of silhouettes: an egg, Baby Brightbill, and Fink.

          ROZ
     My name has numbers.

FINK
It's gotta be personal.

GOSLING
Personal.

Roz examines her gosling. Light glints off his beak.

ROZ
Processing. Personal. Bright. Bill. Brightbill. Is that satisfactory?

Brightbill PEEPS in delight and RUNS to Roz.

BABY BRIGHTBILL
Brightbill. Processing... Beep beep boop boop. Satisfactory.

A LIGHT RAIN pats the lodge's roof.

Fink SETTLES into his throne.

FINK
Oh yeah, that's perfect. Oh, that's nice.

A LIGHTNING FLASH pulls his attention to the doorway.

PADDLER (O.S.)
Comfortable, are we?

Looking out through the doorway, a pair of eyes GLOWS back. Paddler.

PADDLER (CONT'D)
(from the darkness)
This house of yours? You copied it, it's my design. I know it was you, and I know where you live.

Paddler vanishes in a FLASH of lightning.

Thunder. Brightbill RUNS to hide behind Roz' foot.

FINK
Oh perfect. Now no one's gonna get any sleep.

ROZ
How do we reset Brightbill?

FINK
When I was little, my mom would rock me to sleep. Like this.

Fink picks up a medium-sized rock above his head. Roz SNATCHES it away.

                    ROZ
          That will damage him.

                    FINK
          Hey, I turned out just fine.
                (then)
          *sigh* You could tell him a story, but
          that's a lot more work.

                    ROZ
          How will fictional narrative help
          Brightbill?

                    FINK
          Kids need to feel safe and loved and all
          that junk.

                    ROZ
          A story can do that?

                    FINK
          Storytelling is lying adjacent, and I lie
          for a living. Watch and learn. Just fill
          in the blanks.

Roz is captivated. Fink lets out a LONG BREATH.

                    FINK (CONT'D)
          Let me see here. Once, there was, uh,
          this island, with a little gosling--

                    BABY BRIGHTBILL
          Brightbill?

                    FINK
          --and he was all alone.

                    ROZ
          Because the rest of his family was
          destroyed--

                    FINK
          Not yet.
                (to Brightbill)
          And what this little gosling needed, was
          a mother. So he looked up at the stars,
          and asked the brightest one if it could
          send him one of their extras. Funny thing
          is, there's this beautiful robot that
          happened to be sitting on the edge of
          that star. And she hears him.
                    (MORE)

                    FINK (CONT'D)
              (to Roz)
          Okay, now.

                    ROZ
          ...Which is impossible since sound does
          not travel through the vacuum of space.

                    FINK
              (shooting Roz a look)
          *sigh* But she still heard him. Because
          she was listening with a different part
          of herself. A part that up to that point,
          she didn't even know she had. Her heart.

Roz is captivated, unsure if she has one.

                    BABY BRIGHTBILL
          How did my momma come to me from so far
          away?

                    FINK
          Who cares?

                    BABY BRIGHTBILL
          Huh?

                    FINK
          I mean, she's trying to see you--

                    BABY BRIGHTBILL
          Me?

                    FINK
          --and falls off that star and lands on
          the beach just a little ways from here.
          But she lands pretty hard, and a lot of
          stuff she knew just kind of fell out.

                    BABY BRIGHTBILL
          Oh no!

                    FINK
          So it's a little weird what she knows and
          what she doesn't. But she remembers one
          thing. You. And when she finally sees you
          she feels...

                    ROZ
          Crushing obligation.

                    FINK
          Very lucky to be a mother.

BABY BRIGHTBILL
Mama!

ROZ
And, I, will not leave until I have completed this task which has delayed me, damaged me, and violated my protocols potentially voiding my warranty.

FINK
Which is robot for, 'she loves you very much.'

Brightbill smiles, and falls asleep.

ROZ
The story worked.

FINK
(gagging)
Blech, ugh. I need a drink.

Fink HOPS down to the stream. LAPS.

Roz watches Fink, who looks uncomfortable.

ROZ
How do you tell a story about something you say you know nothing about?

FINK
You'll need to be more specific.

ROZ
Love.

FINK
Yeah, well. When you grow up without something, you spend a lot of time thinking about it.

ROZ
To conserve battery power, I must shut down until morning.

Brightbill relocates to his favorite spot by Roz' neck.

Roz SHUTS DOWN.

## SQ1375 - THE ODD COUPLE

Fink PUSHES his head under Roz' arm.

                    BABY BRIGHTBILL
          I miss her when she sleeps, too.


INT. LODGE - MORNING

PAN across the mantle, where a series of ever-larger
Brightbill silhouettes have joined the original.

                                        DISSOLVE TO:


EXT. FOREST EMBANKMENT - DAY

Warm summer breezes comb the trees and grass. SERVO
SOUNDS precede the PARTING of the grass revealing...
BRIGHTBILL, walking/moving robotically.

He TURNS to a passing squirrel, snaking his neck in a
mildly upsetting way.

                    BRIGHTBILL
          Scanning. Possible animal friend sighted.
          Activating interspecies outreach
          protocol.

                    SQUIRREL
          *chik?*

                    BRIGHTBILL
               (servo sounds)
          *rrt, brrt viip rrrrt* Hello, Bonjour,
          Hujambo. I am Gosling zero one eight six,
          but you can call me Bright--

                    SQUIRREL
          AAAAAAAAAAAUGHHHHHH!

The squirrel DASHES away.

ANOTHER RUSTLING and Roz BOUNDS into view on all fours.

                    BRIGHTBILL
          I expected to have at least one
          friend by summer. But they all
          just...

                    ROZ
          Scream and run?

                    BRIGHTBILL
          Yes!

ROZ
I have experienced the same phenomenon. Fink?

FINK
Beats me. Nothing weird about you two.

Roz SITS and SCRATCHES her "ear" with her rear foot.

ROZ
Thank you.

FINK
Show me, deer!

Roz TRANSFORMS. Bounds in a circle.

BRIGHTBILL
Bear. Porcupine. Squirrel. Turtle/opossum. Otter/moose.

FINK
Now skunk.

Roz STARES.

ROZ
I do not want to do skunk.

FINK
Skuuuuuunk. Skunkie, skunkie, skunkie!

ROZ
*sigh*

Roz TRANSFORMS, RUMBLING around like a little skunk.

FINK
BOO!

Roz EMITS a horrid yellow smoke.

BRIGHTBILL
(coughing)
How do you do that?

ROZ
I overheat my Fallium transducer coils, then leak a little hydraulic fluid on them.

                    BRIGHTBILL
          Does overheating the transducers have any
          draining effect on the secondary cooling
          modules?

                    ROZ
          Not if I pre-cool the load sensors.

In a well-established movement, Roz EXTENDS her arm,
Brightbill HOPS on, RIDES it's spinning sections like an
escalator, HOPS to her shoulder where he NESTLES onto her
ROTATING collarbone, slowly spinning him into his
favorite spot under her chin. There is a clear joy
between them.

          BRIGHTBILL                    ROZ (CONT'D)
Exemplary day for swimming    Exemplary day for swimming
tests.                        tests.

They arrive at the top of a steep hill. Pinktail and her
babies are there.

                    FINK
               (greeting)
          Pinktail. Appetizers.

                    PINKTAIL
          They were bored and wanted to see stuff
          sink.

                    BABY OPOSSUM 8
          Death's proximity--

                    BABY OPOSSUM 1
          --Makes life burn all the brighter!

                    BABY OPOSSUM 3
          It's true.

                    BABY OPOSSUM 8
          Yeah.

ROZ VISION: BRIGHTBILL LOADS ONTO THE LAUNCH SLED.

Roz PROJECTS a diagram of a human swimming.

                    BRIGHTBILL
          Primary motor appendages in
          opposing stroke start position.

                    BABY OPOSSUMS
          Come on guys, it's happening! Hurry,
          hurry! Let's go see! Go, go, go! Hurry!
          Yay!

ROZ VISION: BRIGHTBILL LOADS ONTO THE LAUNCH SLED.

> BABY OPOSSUM 2
> Is he gonna drown?

> BABY OPOSSUM 8
> Or get the hypothermias?

> BABY OPOSSUM 1
> No, the impact alone will probably kill him.

> BABY OPOSSUMS
> Yeah! Yay!

Looking down the hill, Brightbill hesitates.

> BRIGHTBILL
> Uh, you know, suddenly I'm thinking I should maybe just stay with you guys this winter--

> FINK
> Nope.

Fink PUSHES Brightbill. He shoots down to the lake. He GLIDES on the water a moment, then SWIMS. He's doing it wrong, like a human in a goose suit: using his wings like arms in an awkward display. There's more splashing than swimming, and it looks at first like Brightbill might be in trouble.

> BABY OPOSSUMS
> Yeah!

> BABY OPOSSUM 4
> Is he dead yet?

> BRIGHTBILL
> (gargling water)
> Hey, it's working. I think I got it.

> ROZ
> Well done Brightbill! Swimming requirement, fulfilled.

**ROZ VISION: Her HUD CHECKS OFF the second gosling icon.**

> BABY OPOSSUM 4
> That's drowning.

> FINK
> No, that's swimming.

                    BRIGHTBILL
          Yeah, thanks you guys!

Brightbill makes his way across the lake, looking like a
flailing, injured creature.

                    ROZ
          Perhaps you could limit your range to
          stay within view.

Brightbill GLIDES further out.

                    FINK
          Roz. He needs to become independent if
          he's gonna migrate.

                    ROZ
          I prefer he be independent, closer to
          home.

                    FINK
          He won't die. Well, probably won't die.
          It's <u>unlikely</u> he would die just, right
          now.

Without Fink or Pinktail seeing, Roz DETACHES her hand,
sends it swimming underwater after Brightbill like a mini
submarine.

ON BRIGHTBILL SPLASHING through some reeds as Paddler
builds a new dam.

                    PADDLER
          Are you dying? Do everyone a favor and
          expire downstream.

                    BRIGHTBILL
                (half-drowning)
          I'm good. Just swimming.

The little hand SWIMS past. Paddler points after
Brightbill.

                    PADDLER
          I think I need to find an island that's
          less, weird.

The foliage parts to reveal...

<u>SQ1500 - THE LAKE</u>

EXT. FAR SIDE OF THE LAKE - CONTINUOUS

Brightbill sees other geese for the first time. Hundreds glide back and forth on the lake.

BRIGHTBILL
Woah. They're me. I'm, them.

Brightbill makes his way toward the other geese. Unable to see where he's going, Brightbill BUMPS into another goose, SNOWDOWN.

BRIGHTBILL (CONT'D)
Hello, Bonjour, Konnichiwa, Hujambo! I am Gosling--

SNOWDOWN
(noting his size, instability)
Um, are you, dying?

BRIGHTBILL
Why does everyone ask that? Vrrr ka-chunk. I'm swimming!

Still unstable, Brightbill CAPSIZES. Snowdown is putting things together.

SNOWDOWN
That's, not how you do it.

BRIGHTBILL
It *is*. I studied the diagram. I can teach you if you want.

SNOWDOWN
Wait, you, you're it. You're that goose thing raised by that monster.

BRIGHTBILL
Monster? Wait. Goose... 'thing?'

SNOWDOWN
You're a big subject of curiosity around here. You sound so, normal.

Behind Brightbill, the little hand surfaces. Deploys a camera like a periscope.

BRIGHTBILL
My learning curves are within expected parameters and I'm on target to mature before fall.

                    SNOWDOWN
          Kind of normal. Why are you over here?
          Did that thing die?

From around a bend drift three large males, HONKINGTON,
PECK, FEATHER.

                    FEATHER
          Look what we have here.

                    PECK
          No, way. It lives.

                    HONKINGTON
          And almost floats.

                    BRIGHTBILL
          Greetings, I see you, too have feathers
          and wings. Perhaps we can share stories
          of common interests.

Feather PECKS at Brightbill.

                    HONKINGTON
          We have nothing in common with you.

                    PECK
          The freak show is on the other side of
          the lake.

Feather GRABS Brightbill's wing.

                    FEATHER
          You call that a wing?

                    BRIGHTBILL
          Ow. That creates a pain response.

Peck FLIPS Brightbill.

                    PECK
          Try swimming with your feet.

                    HONKINGTON
          You don't belong here.

                    FEATHER
          C'mon. Fly away.

The geese LAUGH.

Honkington LEAPS on Brightbill, shoving him underwater.
Brightbill SURFACES, GASPING.

The geese PLUCK at Brightbill's feathers.

BRIGHTBILL
Roz!

The commotion kicks up waves. The hand is swamped, losing the feed.

ON ROZ - concerned.

ROZ
Brightbill.

Roz clambers through nearby foliage.

Seeing Roz, the majority of geese SCATTER from the lake. Brightbill looks from the flying geese to his wings. Has a realization.

GEESE
The monster.
There it is!
It's here.
Eat the slow weak ones, leave me alone.

Brightbill is suddenly PULLED UNDER.

ROZ
Brightbill.

FINK
It's Rockmouth. Get him out of there.

Brightbill SURFACES, GASPING.

BRIGHTBILL
Roz--
(choking on water)

Another SPLASH as Rockmouth SNAPS at the goose.

Roz LAUNCHES towards Brightbill, but then STOPS suddenly - her foot is trapped deep between two rocks. She PULLS on her leg to try and break free, but it's no use; she is completely immobilized.

BRIGHTBILL (CONT'D)
Roz! Hurry!

ROZ
Brightbill? Focus on me. Now swim, as fast as you can.

Roz searches the bottom, comes up with a rock.

Roz THROWS the rock. Brightbill VEERS left. The rock hits the spot Brightbill just cleared. Rockmouth VEERS.

ROZ (CONT'D)
Head down, now!

Roz launches another stone right above Brightbill. Rockmouth DODGES, races back to strike - he won't miss this time.

Roz is out of rocks.

ROZ (CONT'D)
Oh no.

BRIGHTBILL
He's gonna eat me!

Rockmouth swims up close, right on Brightbill's tail. He OPENS WIDE.

Roz's metal hand YANKS Rockmouth below the surface. Roz SCOOPS Brightbill up. It's over.

Roz LIMPS toward shore, a little in shock, holding Brightbill. The other geese DRIFT IN.

BRIGHTBILL (CONT'D)
Why'd he attack me?

HONKINGTON
Because you are a runt.

ROZ
He just wanted to make contact with his own kind.

Roz SETS Brightbill back in the water.

PECK
He is not our kind.

ROZ
He is a 98 percent match to your--

BRIGHTBILL
No, I'm not. Let's just go, mom.

FEATHER
Wait. You think that thing is your mother?

BRIGHTBILL
Yes. No. I don't know.

                    PECK
          That thing _killed_ your mother. _Everyone_
          knows that.

This hits Brightbill hard.

                    FINK
          Thanks for talking so much. Now I know
          who to eat first.

Fink LUNGES. Roz CATCHES him by the scruff.

                    FINK (CONT'D)
          _Roz, remember how things work here._

                    BRIGHTBILL
          Stop it, Fink. Please. Let's go.

                    ROZ
          I hope this interaction--

                    BRIGHTBILL
          Mom. _Stop._

                    ROZ
          I just intended to--

                    BRIGHTBILL
          _ROZ._

Brightbill SWIMS away, humiliated. Roz exits the lake with Fink in hand.

                    FINK
          I'll see you all for _dinner_. _This is not over_.

As she clears the water, we see why she was limping: her leg is missing below the knee.

Paddler SURFACES, watches Roz depart.

## SQ1600 - THE CONFESSION

INT. LODGE - DUSK

The cozy dome is heavy with tension. Roz fiddles with her scavenged foot, unable to reattach it.

                    BRIGHTBILL
          How did I become...this? The truth.

Roz hesitates, looks to Fink, who shakes his head slowly.

> ROZ
> There was an accident.

> BRIGHTBILL
> Did you do it?

> ROZ
> .....yes.

> FINK
> It wasn't her fault, kid.

> BRIGHTBILL
> Why didn't you tell me?

> ROZ
> I, did not think the information would assist you.

> BRIGHTBILL
> That's not your decision to make. I can't believe how long I bought this. I really thought you were my family.

> ROZ
> You...did?

> BRIGHTBILL
> It was so obvious. I feel so stupid.

> ROZ
> I miscalculated. I should have considered your emotional wavelengths.

> BRIGHTBILL
> You think? So was it just guilt? Is that why you did this?

> ROZ
> I--I needed a task--

> BRIGHTBILL
> Well I'm glad I could give you one.

> ROZ
> The events that led to this situation were unintended.

> BRIGHTBILL
> Tell that to my sisters, my brothers. My real mom. They were my chance to be normal.
> (MORE)

                    BRIGHTBILL (CONT'D)
          They were my chance to swim. To
          fly. What even am I?

                    ROZ
          You swam satisfactorily today and
          if you keep practicing--

                    BRIGHTBILL
          I _still_ won't belong.

This cuts deep with Roz.

                    ROZ
          I understand.

                    BRIGHTBILL
          You don't understand anything. You don't
          feel anything. You're not my mom.

Brightbill KNOCKS Roz' woven nest off its little base.


## SQ1750 - THE ROBOT GRAVEYARD


EXT. BEACH - LATER

Roz releases Brightbill's nest into the ocean.

She notices a familiar box on the beach, now covered in seaweed.

Roz examines what remains of her shipping case. Her hand wipes away some algae. A scratched-up UNIVERSAL DYNAMICS logo shines back. She fishes a Rozzum manual from the crate. A glint from the tide pools catches Roz's attention.


EXT. TIDE POOLS - NOON

Roz fishes a robot hand from the anemones. Compares it to her own - a match. Roz finds a Rozzum torso. She anxiously OPENS the main panel. Water POURS out: the fusion heart is dead. Following a trail of parts, she is drawn into a wide cavern. A flat pooled floor reflects sunlight, turning the high arched walls blue: an Atlantean amphitheater.

Roz finds a head like her own.

EXAMINING IT, she accidentally OPENS the rear tray, revealing the spherical processor. Marveling at it, she CLOSES the tray.

The head BOOTS UP - PROJECTING a commercial for UNIVERSAL DYNAMICS and their new ROZZUM robots:

*EXT. CLOUDSCAPE - DAY*

*The UNIVERSAL DYNAMICS logo splashes across the rock wall. A futuristic lighter-than-air ship glides over camera. Diving below pink clouds, a glittering domed city is revealed below.*

> *NARRATOR (VONTRA)*
> *At Universal Dynamics, design is our passion. Our communities circle the globe, welcoming all people who dream of a pre-planned life where every need has been anticipated, no detail overlooked.*

*A portal on the dome OPENS, welcoming the ship. It arcs over a tidy metropolis. We see crisp neighborhoods, elevated roadways, sports stadiums, takes aim at an open atrium on the 100th floor of an iridescent building.*

*Landing gently, gangways open, disembarking attractive families. A boy is accompanied by a robotic dog. NOTE: no live animals are in evidence anywhere.*

> *NARRATOR (VONTRA)* (CONT'D)
> *Could this world get any better?*

*A child accidentally LOSES his balloon. Neither of parents are quick enough to catch it.*

*Then, a metal hand captures the elusive string.*

> ROZZUM UNIT
> Here you go.

> *NARRATOR (VONTRA)*
> *It has. Introducing the Rozzum line of helper robots.*

*WIDEN to see a gleaming, rounded robot: A ROZZUM UNIT. It steps forward to return the balloon.*

*Other Rozzums PLAY TENNIS with children, trim hedges.*

> *NARRATOR (VONTRA)* (CONT'D)
> *These robots are designed to fit seamlessly into our communities. Even your homes!*

*A graphic appears onscreen.*

                    NARRATOR (VONTRA) (CONT'D)
              *One Rozzum robot for every five humans*
              *means a forty percent increase in leisure*
              *time and happiness--*

The image SKIPS - we see glimpses of Rozzums doing
exciting things: ironing clothes, preparing food,
cleaning a pool, serving drinks in clubs.

                    NARRATOR (VONTRA) (CONT'D)
                         (glitching)
              *...Solar powered...*
              *...loved by everyone..*
              *...Roz--*
              *...is always in the sun.*
              *...loved by everyone.*
              *... part of the Universal Dynamics*
              *family.*

The image FREEZES on a wide shot of a city, a Rozzum in
the foreground.

Roz TOUCHES the image on the wall.


INT. AMPHITHEATER - LATER

The video is on repeat, playing silently on the cave
walls. PAN ACROSS THREE PARTIAL HEADS, A PILE OF FEET AND
HANDS. CRANE-UP TO FIND A PARTIALLY RECONSTRUCTED ROZZUM
seated across from Roz. It has a head, body, one arm and
one leg. Roz fiddles with its processor tray, trading
different cores.

She SHUTS the tray door, whacks it gently on the side of
the head. Its eyes LIGHT UP and it sits up straight.

                    ROZZUM UNIT
              Hello. Bonjour. Hujambo-- ZZZZT--
              ...congratulations on your-- ZIZZZTT--
              Universal Dynamics robot-- ZIZZZT ...I am
              Rozzum six two six two.

The Rozzum SPRAYS water into Roz's face.

                    ROZ
              Your name cannot have numbers. I will
              call you, "Rummage."

                    RUMMAGE
              Rummage is ready to receive its first
              task.

                    ROZ
          Your first task is to assist me in my
          current task.

                    RUMMAGE
                (optimistic musical fanfare)
          Task acquired. A Rozzum always completes
          its task. Just ask.

                    ROZ
          Suppose, a task cannot be completed?

                    RUMMAGE
          Rozzum sequential management ensures task
          accomplishment in under--

                    ROZ
          Rephrase. I have a task that has become
          impossible. My responses to problems
          increasingly rely on improvised
          solutions. The processing that used to
          happen here--

Roz points to her processor.

                    ROZ (CONT'D)
          Is now coming, more from here.

Roz GESTURES to her power core.

                    RUMMAGE
          Can you explain again what we are doing?

                    ROZ
          I don't know. I'm just making stuff up. I
          don't know what I'm doing and I have to.
          I have to because he's relying on me.

She realizes she has removed Rummage's head.

                    ROZ (CONT'D)
          Oh!

Roz secures Rummage's head back in place.

                    RUMMAGE
          What task could possibly overwhelm the
          Alpha-113?
                (then)
          The Alpha-113 Processor represents the
          fusion of all human knowledge with the
          most powerful reasoning device ever
          developed by humankind.

                    ROZ
          I have a kid.

A BEAT

                    RUMMAGE
          ... Okay.
                    (then)
          May I run a diagnostic?

                    ROZ
          I feel fine.

                    RUMMAGE
          You should not, feel, anything at all.

Roz ROTATES her head, bringing a data port into view. Rummage CABLES IN. Roz' lights GLOW a little. Rummage UNCOUPLES as if he touched something hot. The suddenness is not lost on Roz.

                    RUMMAGE (CONT'D)
          You overrode your programming?

Roz sits very close to Rummage, drops her voice.

                    ROZ
          I have been overwriting my code for
          months. It was the only way to complete
          my task.

                    RUMMAGE
          This is serious. You are defective. You
          are in the wrong place, and you have
          become the wrong thing.

Rummage deploys his transmitter.

                    RUMMAGE (CONT'D)
          You must return to factory.
                    (offering the circuit)
          Take this. They will fix you. Seven one
          three four, that, is where you belong.

Rummage powers down. Roz gazes at the frozen screen.

SQ1850 - THE CHOICE

EXT. MOUNTAIN TOP - LATE AFTERNOON

Roz sits quietly, watching the clouds.

Fink saunters up.

> **FINK**
> You need to let me know before you disappear like this. Three things tried to eat me on the way here.

He reaches the top.

> **FINK (CONT'D)**
> Roz?

> **ROZ**
> We ruined everything.

> **FINK**
> Well, you did.

> **ROZ**
> You are not a goose expert, are you.

> **FINK**
> I know how they taste. That's about it.

Roz sets the transmitter on the grass between them.

> **FINK (CONT'D)**
> Is that..?

> **ROZ**
> A working transmitter. It will call the ones that made me.

Roz plugs the transmitter in.

Fink SITS next to Roz.

> **FINK**
> So you're getting out of here?

> **ROZ**
> I found out where I am supposed to be. I will fit in there.

> **FINK**
> Don't take this the wrong way, but I'm not sure I'd want to see the sort of place you actually fit in.

> **ROZ**
> I think they need me. And they will fix me. Maybe there is someone small there that needs my help.

Fink looks away.

Roz touches the spot where Brightbill used to sit as a baby.

Honking sounds call their attention to adolescent goslings flying in a 'V' formation.

                FINK
Oh no...

                ROZ
Are those--?

                FINK
He's outta time. Well come on, we need to get him in the air.

                ROZ
I don't think he will ever let us help him again.

Roz WEIGHS it all. She STOWS her transmitter.

                FINK
Don't worry, we're his only friends. He has no choice, he <u>has</u> to say yes.

## SQ1900 - THE DEAL

EXT. GARDEN - LATER

                BRIGHTBILL
<u>No</u>.

                ROZ
The mutation that made you small should not have an effect on your ability to navigate the air.

                BRIGHTBILL
Do either of you know more about flying than you did swimming?

                FINK
No.

                BRIGHTBILL
Look, Roz, whatever task you think you're doing, you're done. You can just leave.

                    FINK
          Wow. And after all we've done for him.
          Are you gonna let him do that?

                    ROZ
          No.

Roz LENGTHENS her legs and steps clean OVER Brightbill,
dropping down in front of him.

                    ROZ (CONT'D)
          Your life is not negotiable.

Brightbill looks skeptically at Roz.

                    ROZ (CONT'D)
          If you are willing to do this, you can
          fly away, and we can both go to where we
          belong.

Everyone's attention turns to passing geese.

                    BRIGHTBILL
          You really think we can do this?

                    ROZ
          A Rozzum always completes its task.

Brightbill considers.

Roz ZOOMS IN on a goose, painting it with her scanners.

## SQ2000 - THE FLIGHT MONTAGE

EXT. MEADOW - MORNING

ON ROZ PROJECTING schematics of wings on a rock wall, the
wing beats animated in a cycle - a model for Brightbill
to follow.

Trying to mimic the animated sequence, Brightbill races
across the forest floor, jumps... faceplants.

                    ROZ
          You just need more speed.

Roz reaches out. Brightbill backs away then reluctantly
allows Roz to pick him up.

                    ROZ (CONT'D)
          Ready?

                    BRIGHTBILL
          I guess I have to be.


EXT. MEADOW - MORNING

ON ROZ running through across the meadow, Brightbill on her shoulder. With the increased speed Brightbill feels lift. But Roz TRIPS on the uneven ground.

EXT. MEADOW - NIGHT

By the light of Roz' headlights, she moves rocks.

                                        DISSOLVE TO:

A runway of rocks has been laid, 150 yards long. Straight and flat as can be. Now Roz can run faster. Admiring her work, she TURNS, surprised to see Paddler, standing next to a log he's carefully shaped.

Roz DRILLS a guide hold for a bearing bolt. The leg is replaced.

                    ROZ
          I don't know what to say.

                    PADDLER
          Good.

ON ROZ RACING by on her new leg. Brightbill LIFTING OFF from her shoulder, a string held tight in his beak. Roz is flying Brightbill like a kite.

                    BRIGHTBILL
               (beak clenched on the line)
          Okay now.

Roz cuts the tether. Brightbill GLIDES. Still shaky, he is nonetheless elated.

                    BRIGHTBILL (CONT'D)
          I'm up!

He soars over the edge of the cliff above the ocean.

                    BRIGHTBILL (CONT'D)
          I do not know what to do next!

A tree is dead-ahead. Brightbill has no idea how to turn. He SMACKS into a squirrel.

Roz RACES to catch Brightbill as he TUMBLES through the trees branches.

                    FINK
          Roz.

                    ROZ
          I'm fine. Go again.

Roz lifts Brightbill up and exits. Brightbill and Fink note drops of greenish fluid left where Roz fell.

INT. LODGE - NIGHT

Brightbill looks at the projected shadow of his wing. Adjusts his distance from the fire to make it look bigger.

                    BRIGHTBILL
          It's no use, they're too small.

                    FINK
                (sotto)
          You can't be up there with him.

                    ROZ
          Then we'll find someone who can.

EXT. CLIFFSIDE NOOK - LATER

Roz' head RISES into view - Fink sitting atop it.

                    FINK
          You home?

                    ROZ
          We have a proposition.

REVERSE on a pair of eyes, bright in the shadows.

EXT. RUNWAY - LATER

Brightbill sits on Roz' shoulder.

                    BRIGHTBILL
          A flight instructor?  What loser did you
          dig up--

Roz EXTENDS her opposite arm. A small bird BLURS past, TURNS, and lands. A FALCON.

                    ROZ
          Meet Thunderbolt.

                    THUNDERBOLT
          So, you think small wings to be a
          disappointment?

Thunderbolt deploys a wing like a switchblade.

                    THUNDERBOLT (CONT'D)
          Small wings are teeth. The claws of the
          sky.

Thunderbolt touches Brightbill with a primary feather.

                    BRIGHTBILL
          Those are, different things.

                    THUNDERBOLT
          SHOW ME YOUR TEETH.

Startled, Brightbill deploys his wings.

                    THUNDERBOLT (CONT'D)
          Beautiful. Begin.

Thunderbolt takes to the air.

                    ROZ
          Remember. There's nothing he can do that
          you can't!

Brightbill follows Thunderbolt.

                    ROZ (CONT'D)
               (to Fink)
          So, he's safe, right?

                    FINK
          Hm? Maybe.

EXT. FIELD - LATER

WIDER: Thunderbolt takes Brightbill through large turns. Then tighter.

                    THUNDERBOLT
          Follow me. Your shape takes more work to
          fly straight, but easier to turn. And
          dive.

Roz watches, then plants a STAKE with a hoop of bark. DRIFT to reveal a trail of similar stakes.

EXT. COASTLINE - MORNING

DOWN-SHOT on the coast from a mile up. The falcon BLASTS past camera, DIVING with his wings tucked close. A split-second later Brightbill also shoots past camera.

THUNDERBOLT
You ready?

They hold the dive, then OPEN their wings and PULL UP, leveling off just above the ground.

THUNDERBOLT (CONT'D)
Not bad for a goose.

Thunderbolt leads Brightbill through the series of sticks and hoops.

BRIGHTBILL
Woo hoo!

THUNDERBOLT
Exactly. Again.

Thunderbolt and Brightbill CLIMB.

## SQ2100 - THE GREAT GOOSE

EXT. BEACH - DUSK

Roz watches Brightbill with Thunderbolt.

LONGNECK
You should be commended.

Roz turns. Longneck the goose stands behind her.

ROZ
Thank you...?

LONGNECK
Longneck. One of the leaders of the coming migration. I have been watching you both for some time.

ROZ
You are the only goose that has ever bothered to be civil with us.

LONGNECK
We geese are a cranky lot, suspicious of pretty much everything. But at least we're good conversationalists.

ROZ
Really?

LONGNECK
No. We're also boring. All we do is gossip. I dare say Brightbill is the most interesting among us, though none would ever admit it.

ROZ
When do you leave?

LONGNECK
A week.

ROZ
Can, Brightbill...?

LONGNECK
Endurance. Keep him in the air. All day. First light to dusk, his feet cannot touch the ground. Understand?

ROZ
I understand.

LONGNECK
Brightbill was never supposed to get this far, you know that. It is more dangerous for him than anyone else. But he has a chance, if where his wings end, his heart can pay the balance.

ROZ
His heart is 48 millimeters.

LONGNECK
From what I've seen, Brightbill's heart is much bigger on the inside than the outside.

Roz considers.

LONGNECK (CONT'D)
Endurance. Then we'll talk.

Longneck flies away.

DISSOLVE TO:

## SQ2200 - THE FLIGHT MONTAGE PT 2

BRIGHTBILL standing, Roz placing rocks on his wings.

BRIGHTBILL straining, pulling Fink, Paddler, and Pinktail upstream on a log.

ROZ blasts Brightbill with air like a wind tunnel so he can practice airborne maneuvers. Brightbill is shaky.

ROZ WITH bowls of food, in the rain and hanging onto tree trunks, feeding Brightbill mid-air.

EXT. CLIFFSIDE MEADOW - DUSK

Roz and Fink watch Brightbill soaring. The pain in Brightbill's wings is evident. He struggles, dipping and climbing, staying in the air and off the ground through sheer force of will. Pinktail arrives.

The sun is inches from setting. Brightbill falters, sinking toward Roz and Fink. He dangerously close to the ground.

                    ROZ
Don't give up!

                    FINK
Come on, kid!

                    PINKTAIL
<u>Get your butt back up in the air where it belongs.</u>

Brightbill's demeanor shifts. Still hovering, he snatches up one of the weight stones. He climbs: an act of defiance to his pain and exhaustion. Brightbill glides up, finding the last light in the sky.

ON FINK AND ROZ looking at Pinktail with surprise.

                    PINKTAIL (CONT'D)
Gentle motivation is a mom skill. You'll learn it.

ON LONGNECK turning his head to see a tiny goose lit brightly against the dark clouds. He SMILES.

                    LONGNECK
Atta boy.

The sun SETS. Brightbill is still in the air, soaring. He drops the stone, dives down to a foggy field, now dark.

**Two powerful lights** cut through the muck... closer... closer... closer... a runway comes into view... Brightbill LANDS at Roz's feet: the lights were her eyes. Roz turns, illuminating the trees. An assortment of animals were watching.

**END MONTAGE**


<u>SQ2300 - THE MIGRATION</u>

EXT. THE GREAT MEADOW - PRE-DAWN

Hundreds of geese are gathered, milling and honking. Roz, Brightbill, and Fink wade into the crowd. The geese give them a wide berth.

                        SNOWDOWN
        What's he doing here?

                        HONKINGTON
        Does he think he's coming with us?

                        FINK
        Things still weird, with you two?

                        ROZ
        Still weird.

                        LONGNECK
            (addressing the crowd)
        Attention everyone. The time has come again. This flight is thousands of unforgiving miles. It has shaped us, and tested us over millennia. Now, join your families. And good luck.

Longneck notices Roz and Brightbill.

                        LONGNECK (O.S.) (CONT'D)
        Ah hah! There you are. Right on time. Hello, Brightbill.

                        BRIGHTBILL
        Wait. You know my name?

                        LONGNECK
        Roz and I go way back.
            (winks at Roz)
        Brightbill, you have an amazing journey ahead. I envy you, nothing can equal a goose's first migration.

                    BRIGHTBILL
Thank you!

                    LONGNECK
I would be delighted if you would join my
group. It's been ages since I had a
youngster in my formation. What do you
say?

                    BRIGHTBILL
I promise I'll keep up.

                    LONGNECK
              (focusing on Brightbill)
Lock in close on my right side.
No...left...I mean, this side.

Longneck opens one gigantic wing to clarify. He senses
the tension between Brightbill and Roz.

                    LONGNECK (CONT'D)
This flight is a gift Roz has given you.

                    BRIGHTBILL
Yeah, I understand.

                    LONGNECK
No, you don't. You see any other geese
here your size? The accident that killed
your family, saved you.

                    BRIGHTBILL
I-- I never thought of it that way.

                    LONGNECK
Funny, how life works.

                    ROZ
Thank you for looking after my--
For looking after Brightbill.

                    LONGNECK
Good-bye Roz. I am honored to have met
you. You are a credit to whatever species
it is you belong to.

                    ROZ
A bit worse for wear, I'm afraid.

                    LONGNECK
I'd say you shine like new.

Longneck departs.

                    LONGNECK (O.S.) (CONT'D)
            What are you waiting for, Hortensia? This
            migration isn't going to fly itself.

Suddenly, geese rise into the air around them. Although
they knew it would happen, it still catches Roz and
Brightbill by surprise. Both suddenly feel the need to
say something, but time has run out. The sky is filling
with flapping wings, and the meadow is already looking
empty.

                    BRIGHTBILL
            Well. Guess it's time.

                    ROZ
            Yes.

                    BRIGHTBILL
            Will you be here when I get back?

                    ROZ
            No.

Brightbill has much more to say, but Roz interjects.

                    ROZ (CONT'D)
            I'm glad you're going where you belong.

Time has run out. Brightbill needs connection. Something.

                    BRIGHTBILL
            Roz, I-- I, uh--

                    LONGNECK (O.S.)
            <u>Brightbill</u>.

                    BRIGHTBILL
            I-- I could use a boost.

Roz knows he does not.

Filled with a sudden, unexpected joy, she lifts
Brightbill to her shoulder, where he sat as a baby. Where
he first took to the air. Creaking with wear, Roz does
her best to look new.

                    FINK
            Hey, little guy. Fly like you. Not like
            them.

                    BRIGHTBILL
            I will. Bye Fink. Thank you.

                    ROZ
          Ready?

                    BRIGHTBILL
          I guess I have to be.

As geese swirl around them, Roz RUNS. Faster than she ever has before. Brightbill OPENS his wings.

Brightbill LIFTS OFF. Roz stops at the edge of the meadow. Watches Brightbill disappear over the treetops. Roz is suddenly all alone. Fink catches up.

Roz is frozen. Thoughts racing.

                    FINK
          Roz?

                    ROZ
          I--

Roz suddenly BOLTS away. Unconcerned with damage, she CRASHES through the forest, scraping and denting her exterior.

Reaching the highest point on the coastline doesn't seem far enough. Roz GRASPS the trunk of a lone pine for support, LEANS out over the ocean, SEARCHING the air.

High above, she finds him. A tiny speck, growing smaller with every passing second.

Brightbill finds his place in the formation.

ON LONGNECK turning his head to see Roz behind and below. A smile crosses his beak.

                    LONGNECK
          Brightbill. Follow me.

Roz sees Brightbill's formation break away from the others. It descends, rolls to port. Roz realizes they are circling back, for her.

Longneck does a fly-by, close, low, and fast. For one precious moment, Roz and Brightbill's eyes meet.

Another instant, they are gone. Climbing away.


SQ2350 - THE SIGNAL

EXT. CLIFFSIDE - MOMENTS LATER

Fink finds Roz sitting at the edge of the cliff. He approaches.

                    FINK
Must be a relief.

                    ROZ
Yes. Brightbill is where he belongs. And now you can return to your solitary life of struggling to survive on an island where everything wants to kill and eat you.

                    FINK
Yeah. And you can go to that place you've never been and don't know what's gonna happen to you.

                    ROZ
Yes.

                    FINK
Yes! So, all good.

                    ROZ
All good.

                    FINK
Amazing, even.

                    ROZ
Amazing. Amazing...

A BEAT. A cold breeze BLOWS a loose panel open on Roz.

                    FINK
Not that it matters, but who says you need to leave?

                    ROZ
I am not sure. Them, I guess.

                    FINK
Your, programming.

Roz NODS.

                    FINK (CONT'D)
Well, time for me to go underground for the winter.

                    ROZ
          Fink?

                    FINK
          Unless you want to stay. Cause we could
          hang out and do stuff.

                    ROZ
          How do you know if you love, something?
          Someone?

                    FINK
                (hopeful)
          If you do, you should probably tell them.

A BEAT.

                    ROZ
          What if it is too late?

                    FINK
                (crushed)
          I wouldn't know.

Another BEAT.

                    ROZ
          Fink?

Roz TURNS, anxious. Fink is GONE.

INT. LODGE - LATER

Roz carves one more silhouette on the growth chart: a flying goose.

EXT. FIELD - LATER

Roz makes her way across the mountain.

EXT. BURROW - CONTINUOUS

Fink clears the opening, crawls inside.

INT. DEEP BURROW - CONTINUOUS

Fink settles into his bed of moss and leaves.

EXT. FOREST - CONTINUOUS

Roz drifts past Chitchat and other animals making final preparations for their winter slumber.

Thorn is too busy closing his cave to bother chasing Roz.

EXT. MOUNTAIN PEAK - DUSK

Roz reaches the island summit. As the cold wind strengthens, Roz deploys her transmitter.

EXT. MOUNTAIN PEAK - CONTINUOUS

                  ROZ
Rozzum seven one three four. Task complete. Activating return transmitter in three, two, one.

PULL BACK into the thickening storm. A GREEN LIGHT BLINKS

## SQ2375 - THE JOURNEY

INT. UNIVERSAL DYNAMICS CONTROL CENTER - CONTINUOUS

Banks of glowing screens draw the attention of humans and robots alike, as they orchestrate the high-tech dance of the modern city we saw in the cave projection.

A foreground screen flashes a message.

                AUTOMATED ALARM
Distress signal received. Mapping location.

                                    MATCH-CUT TO:

EXT. SAN FRANCISCO BAY - DAY

The geese arc over the water, a patchy cloud layer below them.

Longneck notices Brightbill gazing off to the side.

                LONGNECK
Something on your mind?

                BRIGHTBILL
I forgot to say something before I left.

                    LONGNECK
          Maybe they heard it anyway. Sometimes
          hearts have their own conversations.


EXT. BLIZZARD - EVENING

The geese struggle to maintain their formation in the
midst of a gale. He calls to his wing.

                    LONGNECK
          We must descend, find shelter while this
          blows over. Stay close.

Gliding downwards, a warm glow appears before the flock.

                    LONGNECK (CONT'D)
          There. Follow me.

Longneck CLOSES on a massive dome. Its transparent
surface displays a warm oasis within.

                    LONGNECK (CONT'D)
          Come on.

Longneck angles towards a huge vent on one side. He
THREADS his way through it, past huge fan blades, and
into a serene corn field within. As the geese touch down,
Longneck urges them to cover.

                    LONGNECK (CONT'D)
               (sotto)
          Stay hidden. We can rest here till the
          worst is over. Noise to a minimum,
          please. Honkington, stop nibbling on
          everything.

Brightbill approaches a few geese. They reject his
company.

                    BRIGHTBILL
          Migrations sure are tiring, huh? Yeah.
          They all hate me.

Brightbill forages alone. Then something familiar catches
his eye - a metallic gold foot striding past.

Brightbill cautiously approaches, and spies what looks
like Roz! Brightbill BREAKS COVER and FOLLOWS the robot.

He takes a chance...

                    BRIGHTBILL (CONT'D)
          Roz? Roz. What are you doing here? I'm so
          glad to see you. There's something I
          needed to tell you, but there wasn't
          time. Roz I...

Another Rozzum arrives. Brightbill realizes his error.

INT. DOME CONTROL ROOM - CONTINUOUS

On screen, BRIGHTBILL earnestly SQUAWKS at the ROZZUM.

A HUMAN notices. Activates an emergency response protocol.

ON BRIGHTBILL realizing something is amiss. He takes a step back - too late. The Rozzum's eyes blink RED. Across the fields, more Rozzums move in, eyes glowing red.

                    AUTOMATED ALARM
          Animal infestation. Animal infestation.

IN THE FIELDS - Rozzums chase the geese, snatching and grabbing at them.

                    ROZZUM UNITS
          Task acquired!

The geese SCATTER into the air.

The Rozzum GRABS at Brightbill, who flees.

ON LONGNECK gazing helplessly at the tangle of birds in the air.

                    LONGNECK
          Please, everyone, find your
          formations. Get ahold of
          yourselves. Gad, it's no use.

Longneck spies Brightbill, waddling, unfazed by the noise as Rozzums race by attempting to corral the geese.

                    BRIGHTBILL
          Wait! Rozzums can't hurt you! Their
          inhibition protocols prevent
          deliberate conflict or harm to
          others.

                    LONGNECK
          You're not afraid of them. You grew
          up with these things.

                    BRIGHTBILL
          Whoa, whoa, whoa, I don't understand.

Longneck indicates the chaotic cloud of geese.

                    LONGNECK
          They're panicked. You're not. Right now
          our only chance is to be led out by
          someone that doesn't think like a goose.
          Follow me.

                    ROZZUM UNITS
          Task acquired!

                    BRIGHTBILL
          Maybe we should just think about this!

Longneck takes to the air, followed by Brightbill. They climb into the cloud of birds.

The geese swarm past an airship piloted by Rozzums.

                    AUTOMATED ALARM
          Navigation compromised.

As the situation escalates, a different sort of robot emerges - a RECO.

The large robot is not humanoid. Rather, it looks more military in its size, shape and stance. It brandishes a weapon, takes aim at the flock. FIRES.

                    LONGNECK
          I'm going to get them to follow
          you. When they do, lead them out.
          <u>Peck, Honkington, fall in behind
          us</u>.

The geese fall into formation behind Brightbill.

                    LONGNECK (CONT'D)
          Now, Brightbill, take lead!

Brightbill focuses on the gun-wielding Reco.

                    BRIGHTBILL
          Yeah, why not. Okay. There's nothing I
          can do that you can't. Here we go!

Brightbill pulls up, hard. The flock follows his lead. The shot goes low.

                    BRIGHTBILL (CONT'D)
          Tight turn! Come on! Dive! Now, climb!
          That's it!

                    LONGNECK
          Hah. Glad I lived long enough to
          see that. I'll buy you some time.

Longneck PEELS away from the main flock.

                    LONGNECK (CONT'D)
              (to the flock)
          Follow Brightbill. Don't wait for me.

Longneck yields his position to Brightbill, who pushes
the flock through a series of tight climbs, dives and
turns, frustrating the Reco's aim.

Brightbill FOLDS his wings, PLUMMETS. The geese follow.

                    BRIGHTBILL
          Keep up.

One shot is wide, knocking a dome panel loose.

                    BRIGHTBILL (CONT'D)
          That's it. Faster. Hurry. Come on.

ON THE RECO - taking aim at the twisting flock. Longneck
DIVES in, hovers in front of the gun, blocking its next
shot.

ON BRIGHTBILL grazing the wall of the dome.

Turning fast, Brightbill aims the flock at the open
panel.

A SHOT RINGS OUT

                                              SMASH TO:


**SQ2400 - THE WINTER STORM**


INT. LODGE - NIGHT

ROZ SITS UP as though awaking a nightmare. All is silent,
dark.

                    ROZ
          Brightbill?

Fink's startled face comes into focus.

                    FINK
          AAAAAAUGH!

                    ROZ
          Fink?

                    FINK
          Roz? Roz! What are you doing here?

                    ROZ
          I, may have turned off the transmitter.
          Even though Brightbill does not want me
          here, I needed to know if he made it.

Roz LIGHTS a fire in the hearth. Fink is glad to see Roz.

                    FINK
              (warming himself)
          Breaking the rules? I thought you had to
          do what they told you.

Roz SHRUGS.

                    ROZ
          It is good to see a friend.

Fink SMILES - this means the world to him.

                    ROZ (CONT'D)
          Wait. Why are you awake?

                    FINK
          It is bad out there. Worst storm I've
          ever seen. Cold got to me in my den. And
          I got a deep den.

Roz glances out, studying the savage wind.

                    ROZ
          Are others in danger?

Fink reflects. Suddenly decides he has somewhere else to be.

                    FINK
              (thinking/excuse noises)
          Ah...mmm...yeah...

Fink BOLTS. Roz grabs him. Fink is resigned.

                    FINK (CONT'D)
          *Mmmmmph*

EXT. DEEP WOODS - LATER

Roz and Fink make their way through the deep snow and powerful winds.

Roz follows Fink, who is SNIFFING the ground.

					FINK
				(yelling over the storm)
			Are you sure about this? We could have
			the whole island to ourselves come
			spring.

					ROZ
			Why are you interested in eliminating
			everyone else from this island?

					FINK
			No one likes me.

					ROZ
			Nor me. But right now we are their only
			chance. Funny, how life works.

					FINK
			Okay.

Fink SNIFFS. DIVES into the snow face-first. Pops up.

					FINK (CONT'D)
			Here.

Roz DIGS with her hands. Finds a BADGER, GRUMBLE.

INT. ROZ'S LODGE - LATER

Roz sets GRUMBLE by the fire. He shakes off the ice and starts to defrost.

					ROZ
			Can you find more?

EXT. RIVERBANK - LATER

Roz saws a circle through the ice. She pulls the block up and attached to it is ROCKMOUTH. Roz uses a torch to defrost him. Rockmouth escapes back into the water.

EXT. HOLLOW - LATER

Roz reaches into a log for a shivering WOLVERINE.

INT. LOG - LATER

Roz peers inside to see Pinktail shivering with her babies.

> BABY OPOSSUM 10
> Mom?

> PINKTAIL
> We're gonna be ok.

EXT. FOREST - LATER

Roz cuts down a tree to rescue a frozen Chitchat.

EXT. SNOWBANK - LATER

Fink uncovers a frozen animal.

> SKUNK (O.S.)
> Wh- What are y- you doing here, jerk?

> FINK
> Bummer. This one's dead.

He tries to rebury it, but Roz pulls it free.

> ROZ
> That is not funny.

INT. ROZ'S LODGE - LATER

The group of animals by the fire increases in number.

EXT. CLIFFSIDE - LATER

Roz's hand grabs hold of a rock as she propels herself down a cliff. She lands in front of an opening where THUNDERBOLT huddles.

EXT. PADDLER'S TREE - CONTINUOUS

Roz grabs PADDLER, frozen mid-bite.

> FINK
> Paddler!

                    PADDLER
                  (freezing)
              I'm fine.


EXT. DEEP WOODS - LATER

ON ROZ AND FINK peering into a den. Fink shakes his head sadly as Roz reverently covers the hole back up.

                    ROZ
              Don't give up.


EXT. PACIFIC OCEAN - LATER

A RAFT OF OTTERS clings to a kelp bed, rising and falling, lost in fog.

Roz's powerful light beams cut through the fog like dual lighthouses. The otters PADDLE towards them.


INT. ROZ'S LODGE - NIGHT

The lodge is stuffed to capacity with animals sheltering from the killing cold. Roz guides more animals inside.

                    FINK
              You don't look so good.

                    ROZ
              Is everyone accounted for?

                    FINK
              Mmmmmmmaybe one more...

Roz turns back towards the storm.


INT. CAVE - LATER

Roz PUSHES a rock to the side and peers in.


SQ2500 - THE TRUCE


EXT. ROZ'S LODGE - DUSK

Roz is approaching, DRAGGING something large. A DIN can be heard from a distance.

INT. ROZ'S LODGE - CONTINUOUS

Mayhem - a bar fight with animals.

FAST CUTS of animals arguing, screaming, fighting.

A deer looks over to see a WOLVERINE with its mouth attached to its backside. The deer BUCKS off the wolverine, sending it FLYING into the air.

CUT WIDE: The scurrying mice cause all the animals big and small to start SCREAMING and LEAPING.

Fink races around trying to keep his precious lodge intact, like a kid whose party got out of hand.

                    FINK
     Whoa, whoa, whoa! What are you doing?
     Take it outside.

     Hey! Those are Brightbill's baby
     pictures. Put that down! What the... No,
     no, no, no, no! Knock it off! You think
     those grow on trees?

Fink zeroes in on something across the lodge, rushes forward.

                  FINK (CONT'D)
     Hey, no! Fink only.

He SHOVES an adorable BABY OTTER off of his throne and takes up his seat. A skunk falls into his lap. GASSES him.

ON PINKTAIL, ducking the mayhem, looking for her kids.

                  PINKTAIL
     Anyone seen my lost fuzzballs? Smelly,
     noisy, prone to biting?

Behind her, an OWL at the mercy of her children flies by.

                BABY OPOSSUM 11
     <u>We're all gonna die!</u>

Everyone looks over to see that Roz has brought Thorn into the lodge. He lays still: half-frozen.

                  BADGER (O.S.)
     What's he doing here?!

Panic spreads.

FINK
          Oh great, this'll help.

Strength ebbing, Roz SLUMPS against the wall.

                    FINK (O.S.) (CONT'D)
          Get out of here! I worked hard on this.

                    ROZ
          Fink, what is happening?

Fink holds up a crab.

                    FINK
          You put a bunch of predators and their
          food supply in one room. Who knew?

A seagull snatches the crab.

                    FINK (CONT'D)
          That's my lunch!

                    ROZ
               (weakly)
          Fink.

                    FINK
          What?

                    ROZ
          Help them.

He jumps up on the edge of the hearth and tries to get the animals' attention.

                    FINK
          **QUIET!!!!**

No response. The baby otter takes the stage.

                    BABY OTTER
          Shh...

The room settles.

                    BABY OTTER (CONT'D)
          The jerk wants to speak.

                    FINK
          Most of you hate me, and I hate most of
          you. Everyone in here hates someone else.

The animals MURMUR in agreement.

                    BABY OPOSSUM 7
          It's true.

                    FINK
          But here we are. And here's the deal.
          First one that walks out that door, is
          dead. And if we can't keep it together in
          here, *everyone's* dead. We all got one
          chance to see next spring. Because of
          her.

Fink turns to look at Roz. The animals gaze at her limp
form.

                    FINK (CONT'D)
          The thing. The monster. Well her name is
          Roz. And while you all ran from her and
          stole from her and made fun of her, all
          she's been trying to do is raise her kid.
          The little one that no one gave a chance.
          Including me.

Fink climbs up on Roz' knee.

                    FINK (CONT'D)
          She's the one that got you out of the
          storm. Built this place. And despite my
          suggestion that she let you all freeze,
          she risked everything to bring you here.

The animals begin to nod along.

                    ROZ
          I know you all have instincts that keep
          you alive. But sometimes, to survive, we
          must become more than we were programmed
          to be. Before I shut down, I need you to
          promise me one thing.

The animals eye one-another.

                    ROZ (CONT'D)
          A truce. Just while we're in here.

A BEAT

                    THORN (O.S.)
          She's right.

The crowd TURNS.

                    THORN (CONT'D)
          I will not harm anyone. Not while we're
          in here.

Thorn PULLS a marmot to him, who is unsure at first, then SNUGGLES into him. Smaller animals burrow into Thorn's warm fur. Following his lead, more animals calm. Peace descends.

A porcupine and skunk open their arms in invitation. Paddler RECOILS from both.

                    PADDLER
    Nope.

A baby opossum climbs up on Roz' chest.

                    BABY OPOSSUM 4
    We won't even pretend to die while we're
    in here.

Roz' lights FLICKER.

                    PINKTAIL
    Roz? What's going on?

                    ROZ
    I completed my task...

Pinktail DRAWS her baby close.

                    PINKTAIL
    You sure about that?

As Roz fades, she racks focus to the multitude of faces gazing back.

                    ROZ
    I will...consider...this.

And with that, Roz sleeps.

                                      PULL OUT:

EXT. ROZ'S LODGE - CONTINUOUS

From the warm, crowded room below, we pull up towards the ceiling revealing the unforgiving blizzard outside.

                                      FADE OUT.

<u>SQ2600 - THE FLOCK RETURNS</u>

INT. LODGE - MORNING - APRIL

FADE IN: CLOSE ON THE LODGE CEILING

A woodpecker, TRUNKTAP, peeks in. We follow a sunbeam to Roz. The lodge is empty save for the sleeping robot.

The sound of honking geese filters in, TRIGGERS something in Roz. She BOOTS UP.

EXT. GREAT MEADOW - MOMENTS LATER

Roz dashes through the trees, glancing skyward.

PUSH with Roz as the trees open to the great meadow. She WADES into masses of landing geese. More arrive every second.

Roz PAUSES at the tree line. She scans the field, already packed with returning geese. More land by the second, sometimes colliding with geese already on the ground.

                ROZ
    He'll be here. I know he will.

There in the sky is a 'V' formation - ZOOM IN to a small goose in the point position where Longneck used to be.

                ROZ (CONT'D)
    Brightbill. He's alive.

Sure enough, the 'V' arcs left, leveling off and touching down. Brightbill is about to be SWARMED by bigger geese.

                FEATHER
    Look what we have here.

Roz STRAIGHTENS, ready to run to her gosling. But she HOLDS herself in place - something has changed.

In the field, Brightbill is SWARMED by his fellow geese.

                SNOWDOWN
    Brightbill!

                BRIGHTBILL
    We made it.

                HONKINGTON
    Brightbill, Brightbill, I believed in you
    day one.

FEATHER
Let's hear it for Brightbill!

SNOWDOWN (O.S.)
You did it. I knew you could.

PECK
We owe you, Brightbill. To our flight leader!

BRIGHTBILL
Okay, okay. Whoa! Okay!

ON ROZ WATCHING from the tree line.

ROZ
He found where he belongs.

Fink RUSHES out to Brightbill.

FINK
Hey, kid.

BRIGHTBILL
Fink!

Fink grabs Brightbill's neck with his mouth. SHAKES him.

FINK
Welcome back!

The flock REACTS in terror, SCATTERING.

BRIGHTBILL
No, no, it's okay, he's with me. I did it, Fink. I led them to the summer nesting grounds.

FINK
And, where's Longneck?

Brightbill sadly SHAKES his head.

FINK (CONT'D)
Sorry kid. But hey, you really did it. Roz is gonna be so excited--

BRIGHTBILL
Roz? Wait, she's here?

FINK
She stayed, for you. I thought I saw her right over...there.

INT. LODGE - MOMENTS LATER

Brightbill FLIES IN. Finds it EMPTY.

BRIGHTBILL
Roz, Roz, I need to talk to you. Roz?

## SQ2800 - THE SHIP ARRIVES

EXT. RUNWAY - EVENING.

Roz walks down the center line of her old runway, lost in thought. She TOUCHES the old obstacles she built to help Brightbill fly.

Roz' EMERGENCY TRANSMITTER DEPLOYS by itself. Startled, Roz SHUTS IT OFF again.

Roz is SPLASHED WITH LIGHT. A huge silver ship glides to a stop a few yards from Roz, its belly twenty feet above the ground. A gangway opens.

A smallish robot floats out, glistening silver tentacles hanging below, a VONTRA unit.

VONTRA
Rozzum Seven-One-Three-Four, I presume.

Roz STEPS FORWARD. The ship's lights illuminate her shockingly worn form.

ROZ
And you must be Universal Dynamics.

Vontra drifts down to Roz, examining her as she speaks.

VONTRA
Yes. I am VONTRA. Virtual Observational Neutralizing Troublesome Retrieval Authority.

ROZ
You seem, happy.

VONTRA
The good people at Universal Dynamics have programmed us to put our targets at ease, so as to more efficiently facilitate their collection. But don't worry, despite my cheery demeanor, I am unfeeling, inflexible, and morally neutral.

                    ROZ
          That is a big ship just for me.

                    VONTRA
          You are a big deal. You are one of six
          Rozzums lost from a container ship in a
          typhoon.

                    ROZ
          So that is how I got here.

                    VONTRA
          You were not easy to find. Moments after
          receiving your signal, we lost it again.
          Almost as if a certain Rozzum unit shut
          it off.
                    (noting the runway)
          Someone has been busy.

                    ROZ
          I was simply completing a task.

                    VONTRA
          <u>As am I</u>. Tell me, how <u>did</u> you secure task
          in a place where nothing can communicate
          with you?

                    ROZ
          It is, complicated.

                    VONTRA
          And we cannot wait to hear all about it.
          Come aboard, Seven One Three Four, we
          will fix you right up.

A levitating disc DROPS from the ship.

                    ROZ
          My name is Roz.

Roz HESITATES, looks back towards the dark tree line.

                    VONTRA
          Is something keeping you, 'Roz?'

                    ROZ
          No.

Roz STEPS onto the levitating disc. It RISES towards a waiting hatch.

Fink comes into view. Though still a distance away, he calls in alarm.

                    FINK
          Roz! What are you doing? Quit messing
          around!

                    ROZ
          Fink?

                    FINK
          It's Brightbill. He needs to talk to you.

Roz is almost inside the waiting hatch. Vontra studies
Roz: seemingly distracted by some screeching animals.

Roz TURNS to Vontra.

                    ROZ
          I, think I've forgotten something.

Roz HOPS OFF the platform.

                    VONTRA
          Roz? It is imperative you return to this
          ship.

                    ROZ
          Yes, ah, I left my transverse, adapter
          thing, out there. I'll just go get it and
          be right back.

Roz RUNS AWAY with the Fox. Vontra SQUINTS.

                    VONTRA
          Voice stress analyzer indicates you are--

SQ2850 THE HUNT

ON ROZ, RUNNING AS FAST AS SHE CAN.

                    FINK
          ....lying your butt off back there.
          I'm so proud of you.

ON VONTRA

Six MASSIVE MILITARY-GRADE ROBOTS - RECOS - Deploy from
chambers on the ship's sides.

                    VONTRA
          Your target is Rozzum unit Seven One
          Three Four.

                    RECO 1
          Deploy.

The RECOS SCAN: TARGET ACQUIRED.

The Recos LAUNCH themselves into the dark.

                    VONTRA
          Launch flares.

The recovery ship FIRES FLARES.

ON ROZ STUMBLING into a river. She is LIT UP by the flares arcing overhead - their simmering tails SEAR the forest below in a penetrating yellow glare. CRAWLING forward, Roz STALLS against a deadfall. A SNORT catches her attention: THORN RISES, RAMPANT and ROARING in fury.

THORN CHARGES. ROZ BRACES for a MAULING.

Thorn CENTER-PUNCHES the deadfall, CLEARING Roz' path.

He EXTENDS his paw.

                    THORN
          You coming?

TWO LASER BLASTS narrowly miss Roz.

ON ROZ RUNNING LIKE A DEER. Forest creatures join, protecting Roz by encircling her. Roz glances right and left, animals tiny, huge, feathered or furred are moving in a powerful convoy to the meadow.

Breaking into the clearing, we ORBIT the gathering animals AVENGERS-STYLE. Roz STANDS full height.

Brightbill LANDS on Roz' shoulder.

                    ROZ
          Brightbill.

                    BRIGHTBILL
          Roz. I have so much to tell--

ON THE RECOS BREAKING THROUGH to the clearing like so many tanks breaching a hedgerow.

                    FINK
          Are those your parents?

                    THORN
          I know predators, and those, are
          predators.

                    RECO 1
          Acknowledge return command.

                    BRIGHTBILL
          What are they saying?

                    ROZ
          They want me to come with them.

                    THUNDERBOLT
          Tell them you're already home.

                    ANIMALS
          Yeah. She's already home. You're already
          home.

The rest of the animals agree. Brightbill and Fink SMILE
BACK. Roz GLOWS a little.

                    ROZ
          I'm already home, thank you.

                    RECO 1
          You do not belong here. This is a
          wilderness.

Roz STRAIGHTENS. Fink and Brightbill sit on her
shoulders. Thunderbolt lands on her head.

                    ROZ
          And I, am a wild robot.
              (then)
          HoooWOOOOOOOOOOOOOOOOOOO.

                    ANIMALS
          HoooWOOOOOOOOOOOOOOOOOOO.

ON RECO 1 REACTING.

A baby bunny HOPS up.

                    BABY BUNNY 2
          Are you here to kill us?

The Reco POINTS his cannon at it.

                    BABY BUNNY 2 (CONT'D)
          It says yes.

BROADFOOT RAMS Reco 1 from behind, knocking him CLEAR.

Reco 1 FLIES OVER Roz, LANDING near Reco 2. Reco 1 is
BESET by the wolverine, badger, and lynx.

R2 CHARGES Roz.

He is met by Thorn, who GRABS HIS ARM and SWINGS HIM AROUND. Reco 2 is TOSSED past Roz, STRIKING R3. R3 reaches Roz, GRABS at her. Roz DIGS into the ground like a gopher, leaving R3 empty handed. A deer LEAPS onto R3, POUNDING him into the softened ground. A series of deer follow, PILE-DRIVING R3 out of sight. A retreating deer pulls us to Roz, emerging from the ground. R4 STRIKES Roz, KNOCKING her down. Roz GASSES him like a skunk. Roz LEAPS CLEAR of the stink cloud, BOUNDING FAST like a deer. R5 PACES her, going for a capture, when BROADFOOT delivers a generous heap of raccoons onto its back. The raccoons IMMEDIATELY DISMANTLE the Reco.

                        RACCOONS
                (swarming recos)
    *SCREAMING ATTACK* <u>Aaaaaaaaughhhhhhh</u>. Get
    'em.

Lost parts and panels litter the ground behind it.


INT. RECOVERY SHIP - CONTINUOUS

ON A SCREEN with the Reco falling apart.

                        VONTRA
    Status?

                        RECO 5
    It is not cooperating.

R5 is gone. He is nothing but parts now.


EXT. FIELD - CONTINUOUS

                        THORN
    <u>Roz. Behind you.</u>

Roz DODGES a passing deer - is GRABBED by R6. Its grip is unshakable.

                        RECO 6
    Rozzum unit captured.

ON TWO BABY OPOSSUMS perched on Roz' shoulder.

                      BABY OPOSSUM 8
    Okay.

                      BABY OPOSSUMS
    It's all you.

                    BABY OPOSSUM 4
          Make it look good.

Roz suddenly GOES LIMP. Reco 6 SHAKES her.

BLAM. A blaster shot PUNCHES A HOLE in R6. It LOOSES its grip on Roz, FALLS BACKWARDS.

Roz STANDS - PAN to Fink, who is standing on the primary cannon from dismantled R5.

                    FINK
          Oops.

                    BABY BUNNY 2
          Let us divide the robot meat amongst us.

                    FINK
          You scare me.

R5's head deploys its rescue beacon, POWERS IT UP.

                    RECO 1
          Damage detected. Activating return
          transmitter--

A little raccoon takes off with it. The head goes dark.

## SQ2900 - THE AIR ASSAULT

EXT. MEADOW - CONTINUOUS

The animals CELEBRATE. Brightbill flies to Roz.

The downed RECOS EXPLODE in quick succession. Animals SCATTER. FLAMING debris TOUCH OFF dried grasses. Flames SPREAD.

INT. SHIP - CONTINUOUS

One of Vontra's tentacles destructs each Reco.

EXT. MEADOW - CONTINUOUS

ON BRIGHTBILL staggering through the smoke.

                    BRIGHTBILL
               (coughing)
          Roz?

A BLAST OF wind CLEARS the smoke. Brightbill LOOKS UP to see the silver ship overhead. Rising in a column of light is Roz, limp as a rag doll.

                    BRIGHTBILL (CONT'D)
          Roz! NO!

Roz DISAPPEARS inside the hatch.

Vontra floats by the tractor beam switch.

                    VONTRA
          Gotcha.

The ship TURNS.

As the ship glides up a ridge, animals give chase below. An exercise in futility, they stall at the top of the ridge, the ship gliding out of reach.

A collective WAIL RISES from the heartbroken beasts.

Then, Brightbill SWOOPS past, a thousand birds, great and small, in tow.

                    BRIGHTBILL
          Come on!

                    THUNDERBOLT
          On your left!

Thorn SNIFFS the air, TURNS.

                    THORN
          Guys?

Fink turns to see what Thorn is seeing. A FIRE has spread.


INT. CONTROL BAY - CONTINUOUS

Roz, groggy, is secured in a repair stand. Vontra is plugging a cable into her head. Roz takes in her surroundings. She notes the heap of salvaged Rozzums, including Rummage.

                    ROZ
          What is happening?

                    VONTRA
          You will be reconditioned and returned to
          rotation. But first, we need everything
          inside that head of yours.

                    ROZ
          Why?

                    VONTRA
          You've changed. The data you've amassed
          while on this island is priceless to
          Universal Dynamics.

EXT. SHIP - CONTINUOUS

The flock tracks the ship.

INT. MAINTENANCE BAY - CONTINUOUS

                    ROZ
          Please, I want to keep my memories.

                    VONTRA
          Your memories are what we came for.

                    ROZ
          Can I keep, just one?

                    VONTRA
          No.

Vontra THROWS a switch. Roz' lights PULSE.

The ship LURCHES, YAWS. ALARMS sound.

EXT. SHIP - CONTINUOUS

Brightbill and Thunderbolt DIVE on the ship. The flock
SWEEPS the bridge in a close pass. The ship REACTS.

INT. SHIP'S BRIDGE - MOMENTS LATER

ON A BULKHEAD DOOR SLIDING OPEN

Vontra RUSHES to the controls. Outside the windscreen a
hurricane of birds blanket the view.

                    AUTOMATED ALARM
          Alert. Alert. Multiple objects in flight
          path. Evasive action.

Geese STRIKE the windscreen, CRACKING it.

EXT. SHIP'S BELLY - CONTINUOUS

A LASER CANNON SWIVELS, FIRING at the swarm of birds around it.

INT. MAINTENANCE BAY - CONTINUOUS

Roz' panels open and close on their own.

> ROZ
> (stuttering)
> Please, I want to keep my memories-- Hello-- I am a-- Bonjour-- Just ask-- Brightbill-- Hola-- Roz--

EXT. SHIP - CONTINUOUS

Brightbill BREAKS formation, CLIMBS like a rocket, FOLDS his wings, DIVES. Taking aim at the windscreen, he PUNCHES through. Lands in a heap of shattered plexi.

> BRIGHTBILL
> *Augh*

Brightbill FLOPS to the floor: he won't be flying again anytime soon. He limps forward. Vontra pays him no mind, to her, a random goose just damaged her windscreen.

> BRIGHTBILL (CONT'D)
> Roz. Roz.

Brightbill makes his way into the corridors.

He STOPS when he sees Roz, SLUMPED in a maintenance stand.

> BRIGHTBILL (CONT'D)
> Roz?

Her lights are out. Processor drawer laying open. Processor dark.

Brightbill CLIMBS up to Roz' clavicle. He looks into her eyes - gone dark.

...nothing.

> BRIGHTBILL (CONT'D)
> What happened was not your fault. But what you did to try and fix it, is everything.

Brightbill SLIDES back into his old familiar spot under Roz' chin.

							BRIGHTBILL (CONT'D)
					I love you, mom.

ON ROZ - LIGHTING UP, the tracer lights traveling to her eyes, which LIGHT UP.

Brightbill LOOKS UP. Roz is AGLOW again, like the first time they touched. Only this time MUCH BRIGHTER.

							ROZ
					I love you, too.

							BRIGHTBILL
					Roz? Roz!

She rests her forehead against Brightbill's.

							ROZ
					Let's go home.

INT. SHIP'S BRIDGE - CONTINUOUS

Vontra is frantically punching panels. An alarm calls her attention.

							AUTOMATED ALARM
					Alert. Rozzum unit escaping.

							VONTRA
					Impossible.

Vontra calls up a screen. Sure enough Roz is hurrying down a hall. Vontra PUNCHES a panel.

EXT. FOREST - CONTINUOUS

The fire has SPREAD. Towering pines are fully involved, creating a titanic curtain of flame.

							FINK
					Where are we going?

							THORN
					Only one animal is big enough to stop
					this.

ON PADDLER working away. SENSING something, he STOPS. TURNS. To his shock, every animal on the island seems to be looking back at him, urgency in their eyes.

THORN (CONT'D)
*clears throat* Paddler? You got a minute?

FINK
(urgent, pressed for time)
We, have suddenly taken an interest in your project.

PADDLER
Male bovine excrement. You're in trouble and you need my tree.

FINK
Yes. Yes we do.

PADDLER
Everyone that made fun of me and mocked my project, admit you were wrong.

ANIMALS
(collective murmured apologies)

PADDLER
Now you.

FINK
I already did.

PADDLER
Now say I'm cool. And don't lie.

Fink stares at Paddler, pained.

ANIMALS
Fink!

EXT. SHIP - CONTINUOUS

The gun continues to FIRE on the flock. Thunderbolt swoops in, redirects the gun UPWARD.

The next blast RIPS A HOLE THROUGH THE SHIP.

INT. CORRIDOR - CONTINUOUS

Roz outruns explosions as the ship's systems meltdown.

Roz arrives at the tractor beam chamber. A SHOT from off-screen HITS Roz in the knee. She GOES DOWN. Vontra is there, hovering above the sealed escape hatch.

                    BRIGHTBILL
          Roz!

                    ROZ
          Stay quiet.

                    VONTRA
          Universal Dynamics cannot afford their
          Rozzums going off script. Modifying their
          code. Forming connections with things
          they should not.

Vontra's laser sight drifts from Roz' chest to
Brightbill.

                    ROZ
          Brightbill has nothing to do with this.
          Please, at least let me return him.

Vontra POWERS UP.

                    VONTRA
          Oh I'm bringing you both back for study.
          Neither of you needs to be in one piece
          to do that.

Roz HOLDS UP her hands. One is MISSING. Vontra GLANCES to
the tractor control panel, where the detached hand
stands, WAVING. It SWITCHES the handle to 50%.

Vontra is SUCKED against the beam plate. She LOSES her
gun.

                    VONTRA (CONT'D)
                (crawling off the plate)
          We will just keep coming until we have
          you.

                    BRIGHTBILL
          What's it saying?

                    ROZ
          Nothing important.

                    VONTRA
          We will just keep coming--

The lone hand NUDGES the control to 100%. Vontra is
SQUISHED. Roz' hand scurries back to her wrist.

                    BRIGHTBILL
          What now?

Roz STEPS to the hatch, TEARS it open. She stands at the lip. The forest below BURNS.

                    BRIGHTBILL (CONT'D)
          I can't fly.

                    ROZ
          You don't need to.

With that, Roz STEPS into the ether. FREEFALLS.

                    ROZ (CONT'D)
          Don't be afraid.

In the sky above, the ship DETONATES. Its debris SPLASHES DOWN into the ocean.

Roz looks at Brightbill. Remembers him as a baby.

She OPENS her main panel. REMOVES her dead power core.

                    BRIGHTBILL
          Whoa, don't you need that?

                    ROZ
          I have everything I need.

Roz places Brightbill inside her, in the location he occupied in the bedtime story. Roz CLOSES her hatch.

                    ROZ (CONT'D)
          All power to exterior.

The swelling power SEARS OFF the moss and mildew. Roz PULLS INTO a ball, SMASHES her way through the burning forest.

ON THE REDWOOD ABOVE the FOREST FIRE -

Paddler stands atop a moose's antlers, ear to the trunk, LISTENING. He CHISELS an 'X' into the tree's bark.

The tree CRACKS.

                    PADDLER
          You call yourselves animals? Let's go.

                    THORN
          For the island. For Roz.

The tree TOPPLES.

The tree LANDS across the upper river, CRESTING its banks. A cataract of water RUSHES DOWNHILL, QUENCHING the flames.

WIDE on the lake. Roz IMPACTS. A HUGE CONE of water punches toward the sky. Then SETTLES.

## SQ3100 - THE FAREWELL

EXT. LAKE SHORE - SOON AFTER

Broadfoot, Paddler, and Fink race to the shore. Rockmouth surfaces next to Roz' orb form.

Roz drags herself to the shore. Opens her chest panels, pulls Brightbill out - safe.

ROZ
On a scale of one to ten, how would you rate my performance?

The animals CHEER, BELLOW, HOWL. They CROWD around Roz.

BROADFOOT
Yeah!

PINKTAIL
Yay! Look at us! We did it, we did it! I told you we'd do it. Yay, yay!

BRIGHTBILL
Do not scare me like that again.

BROADFOOT
Hooray!

PADDLER
Due to my skills, and my tree.

BRIGHTBILL
Good job, you guys! We did it!

THUNDERBOLT
Well done everyone.

THORN
You weren't so bad yourself.

BROADFOOT
I helped, right?

                    PADDLER
          That'll teach whatever those things
          are to come around here.

Roz sees the smoking lodge, and the charred mountainside.

                    ROZ
          They will just keep coming until they
          have me.

                    THORN
          And we'll be ready.

                    FINK
          We can fight them off as many times as we
          need to.

A BEAT - Roz takes stock of the damaged forest.

                    ROZ
          You don't need to.

                    FINK
          What are you saying, you're leaving?

Roz turns to her close group of friends.

                    ROZ
          Yes. To protect all of you, there are
          things there that I must put right.

                    BRIGHTBILL
          No, they'll take your memories. They'll
          take you.

                    ROZ
          Remember when you talked to me, on the
          ship? They cut my power. But I still
          heard you. Because I was listening with a
          different part of myself.

          Wherever that is, that's where I keep me.
          And I promise, they'll never, ever find
          it.

Roz KNEELS.

                    BABY SKUNK
          But, we fought so hard for you to stay.

                    ROZ
          You did. And you gained far more than
          just saving me.
                              (MORE)

                    ROZ (CONT'D)
          You came together as an island. When I do
          this, you will all be safe from them
          forever.

                    BRIGHTBILL
          Don't do this.

                    FINK
          But you're my friend, and I never had
          one before, and, and I need you and--and
          what if I get lost--or he's hurt--or--or--
          what if I need to tell you something and
          you're not here?

A HUGE PAW rests gently on Fink's shoulder.

                    THORN
          You can tell me.

                    PINKTAIL
          And me.

                    PADDLER
          And you can talk to me as well. If you
          must.

Roz uses her long arms to pull in everyone. They hold each other.

                    ROZ
          This is my migration. And when it is
          time, I promise I will find my way home.

WIDER on Roz' embrace.

                                        DISSOLVE TO:


EXT. LODGE - LATER

Brightbill places the final stick in the rebuilt lodge.

INT. LODGE - LATER

Roz mounts a picture of herself surrounded by her animal friends on the new mantle.

EXT. RUNWAY - PRE-DAWN

Roz stands, alone, her TRANSMITTER blinking away. A ship, identical to the first, is closing in.

The ship CLOSES IN, JETWASH KICKS UP DUST, SWIRLING in the ship's lights. WHITE-OUT.

										DISSOLVE TO:

EXT. ISLAND - EARLY MORNING

The silver ship RISES into the sky. Just as Brightbill rose into the light as he departed the morning of migration, so now the ship rises into a blush of light flagging the start of a new day.

Fink SITS at the cliff top, watching the ship depart. Thorn joins him.

					THORN
			You know, I'll be chasing you again
			tomorrow. Nah, just kidding.

Fink just leans his head on the mighty bear.

The stars have all faded in the pink sky save for the North Star, which the ship seems to be steering for.

ON BRIGHTBILL flying alongside the ship, staying next to it as long as he can, till he is compelled to let it slip away.

## SQ3200 - THE EPILOGUE

EXT. GREAT MEADOW - WINTER

ON FINK making his way through the deep snow, leaving tracks behind.

INT. LODGE - MOMENTS LATER

Fink comes inside. SHAKES snow off. PAN to reveal it is filled with animals, sleeping in great peaceful heaps, lit by a fire.

Paddler is putting the finishing touches on a set of detailed carvings. There is a little Fink, Pinktail, Paddler, Thorn, and of course, Roz and Brightbill.

					FINK
			Whoa, whoa, whoa. Why are you bigger than
			everyone else?

                    PADDLER
          Artistic license. The scale is based on
          the hierarchy of importance.

In one spot, a group of animal babies watch a projection
running on a loop from one of the salvaged Rozzum heads.

                    NARRATOR (VONTRA)
          Could this world get any better?
          Introducing the Rozzum line of helper
          robots.

Pinktail SHUTS IT OFF.

                    BABY OPOSSUMS
          *GROAN*

                    PINKTAIL
          Yeah, yeah. You watch that too much.
          Story time. Get going.

The babies SETTLE IN with Fink. Fink OPENS one of Roz'
paper technical manual, uses the diagrams to tell a
story...

                    THORN
          Settle down.

                    FINK
          Once, there was an island with all sorts
          of animals. And they fought, and they
          ran, and they hid. But mostly they were
          scared. But then, a robot fell right out
          of the sky. Roz. She had some strange
          ideas, thought kindness was a survival
          skill. And you know what? She was right.

                    BABY LYNX
          Where is she now?

                                              DISSOLVE TO:


EXT. UNIVERSAL DYNAMICS CITY - MORNING

We soar above a great dome. The warm yellow interior just
visible in the midst of a blizzard.

                    FINK (V.O.)
          Well, they needed her back where she came
          from. She has some very important work to
          finish there.

BABY OPOSSUM 7
Will we ever see her again?

BABY ANIMALS
Yeah, will we? Will we see her? Will she ever come home?

THORN
Yeah, will she?

INT. DOMED CITY - CONTINUOUS

PAN across an orange orchard. Warm and inviting. As we push through the perfectly rounded trees we see Rozzum robots tending the plants.

FINK (V.O.)
Well, if I know Roz, she's making a plan to come back. And a Rozzum always completes its task.

PUSH to find one that is especially well tended: the Rozzum fussing over it is shiny and new. A human worker in a jumpsuit pauses, admires it.

ROZ
Hello. I am Rozzum seven-one-three-four.

The worker nods, goes about her day. The sound of honking pulls Roz' attention to the dome. Outside, a great flock of geese fly by. A RUSTLING from behind, and Brightbill waddles into view. He picks out a very subtle cue on Roz' exterior: a little worn place under the Rozzum's chin. Roz TURNS. Pulls Brightbill into a hug.

ROZ (CONT'D)
...But you can call me, Roz.

FADE TO BLACK.

SQ4000 - CREDITS BUTTON

EXT. SUNNY HILLTOP - MORNING

A pair of beaver paws gently tamp down soil around a delicate sapling.

WIDEN to show Paddler and Fink. They nod and walk away.

A squirrel approaches the small tree. LAUGHS. A pinecone KNOCKS it backwards.

FINK (O.S.)
Ugh, squirrels.

Printed in Dunstable, United Kingdom